THE HAUNTING
OF CAPE COD
AND THE ISLANDS

Also by Barbara Sillery

The Haunting of Louisiana
The Haunting of Mississippi

THE HAUNTING
OF CAPE COD
AND THE ISLANDS

BARBARA SILLERY

PELICAN PUBLISHING COMPANY
GRETNA 2014

The word "Pelican" and the depiction of a pelican are
trademarks of Pelican Publishing Company, Inc., and are
registered in the U.S. Patent and Trademark Office.

Library of Congress Cataloging-in-Publication Data

Sillery, Barbara.
    The haunting of Cape Cod and the Islands / by Barbara Sillery.
        pages cm
    ISBN 978-1-4556-1993-1 (pbk. : alk. paper) — ISBN 978-1-4556-
1994-8 (e-book) 1. Ghosts—Massachusetts—Cape Cod. 2. Haunted
places—Massachusetts—Cape Cod. I. Title.
    BF1472.U6S5345 2014
    133.109744'9—dc23

                                                    2014025692

Photographs by Barbara Sillery unless otherwise indicated

Printed in the United States of America

Published by Pelican Publishing Company, Inc.
1000 Burmaster Street, Gretna, Louisiana 70053

To Glinda Schafer, an extraordinary artist and an extraordinary friend. Thank you for all the years of being there for me.

Contents

Prologue

*In culture after culture, people believe that the soul lives on after death,
that rituals can change the physical world and divine the truth, and that
illness and misfortune are caused and alleviated by spirits, ghosts, . . .
and gods.*

—Steven Pinker, *How the Mind Works*

The intriguing apparitions of Cape Cod, Nantucket, and Martha's
Vineyard form an equal-opportunity troupe. Populating these fog-
shrouded lands are preachers and pirates, sea captains and sailors,
lovers and rogues, witches, glass gaffers, giants, and the innocents
whose birthdays numbered far too few. In my previous two books,
The Haunting of Louisiana and *The Haunting of Mississippi,* I
chronicled the deeply rooted and often quirky mysteries of Southern
folklore. Here on Cape Cod, this peninsula-turned-island, and the
neighboring islands of Nantucket and Martha's Vineyard, Yankee
ghosts are staunch and stubborn. They are here whether you believe
or not: they ride the waves, gallop on horseback, stroll along the
beach, play hide-and-seek, race up hills, dance naked in a cupola,
sweep the decks, pilfer make-up, stop a clock, move chairs, rock
beds, block doors, and rattle windows. They are the history of the
Cape and its islands, woven into myth and legend but steadfastly
steering their ghostly vessels through the treacherous shoals of the
present.

Each of the chapters ends with *lagniappe* (lan yap), a Creole term
for a little something extra. When a customer would make a purchase,
the merchant often would include a small gift. The tradition dates

An anonymous sea captain's wife at the Colonial House Inn in Yarmouth Port.

back to the seventeenth century in France. When weighing the grain, shop keepers would add a few extra kernels. *C'est pour la nappe* (It's for the cloth), they would say, as some of the grains tended to stick to the fibers of the material. In New Orleans, where I lived for more than three decades, lagniappe is an accepted daily practice. It is a form of good will, like the thirteenth rose in a bouquet of a dozen long-stemmed roses. The lagniappe at the end of each chapter offers additional background on the ghost or haunted site—perhaps just enough more to entice you to visit these Cape Cod and island locales and seek your own conclusions.

The Haunting of Cape Cod and the Islands

South Church on Orange Street in Nantucket.

1

Seth Did It

Seth Freeman Swift served as the first minister of the Second Congregational Meeting House Society in Nantucket from 1810 to 1833. Among the twenty-first-century parishioners and staff there is a clear consensus: *he's baaack!*

Fuddy Van Arsdale, a former sexton, was often alone in the church before and after services. Tidying up one evening in the empty church, she heard the front door open. Heavy footsteps trudged forward in her direction. As the footsteps advanced, she waited apprehensively for the stranger to appear, but no figure materialized. To quell her fears, Van Arsdale began to sing a traditional hymn. As her quivering voice reached the end of the first verse, she paused and listened. The footsteps stopped, but the shaken sexton never heard them retreat. She was now a believer: the spirit of the first minister had returned. From that harrowing night on, whenever she entered the building alone, she would stop inside the door and announce, "Hi, Seth. I'm here." Seth never snuck up on her again.

During Seth's tenure, parishioners were Congregationalists; later, they voted to become Unitarians. Seth's simple rectangular meeting hall also underwent modifications, and the island community began to refer to the building with its tall tower as South Church. Seth has had a hard time adjusting.

In the winter, to save on fuel and heating costs, the congregation holds services in Hendrix Hall, the smaller, lower-level sanctuary below the cavernous main worship space. Seth's portrait hangs on the left-hand wall, making the ghost of South Church easy to recognize. His auburn hair is brushed forward, framing a long, lean face with

The front doors of South Church opened to let in Seth's ghost.

Portrait of minister Seth Swift, who haunts the church and bell tower.

a square chin. Under his chin, two starched, white, rectangular collars are precisely aligned over a black double-breasted frock coat. When the choir stands to sing "Amazing Grace," the image of Seth is shoulder to shoulder with the group, as if he is lifting his voice with theirs. Pale gray eyes stare out from behind gunmetal gray glasses. It is a portrait of a man keenly aware of every nuance. After the service, when a photographer snaps a picture of Seth's portrait, a male member of the choir approaches and warns, "Watch out! He'll haunt your camera."

Bob Lehman is a jovial and gregarious thirty-year member of the Unitarian Universalist Church. "I've heard all about Seth. The old sextons told stories about being here at night, and they'd hear people walking upstairs, but when they'd check, they couldn't find anyone." Lehman pokes fun at himself: "Seth is an old ghost, you know. He doesn't approve of everything we do. I have not run into him, but then, I'm afraid of the dark, so I don't come here at night." Lehman

The vestry window on which Seth and the boys pounded to gain admittance.

beams, and his blue eyes sparkle. "Seth is everywhere; he has taken on a life of his own." While Lehman adopts a nonchalant attitude about the church's resident ghost, some of Seth's methods for making his presence known have been challenging to deal with.

The duties of a sexton in a Universalist church include cleaning, maintenance, and repairs. One sexton going about his work at South Church had reached his limit with Seth and his ghostly antics—he feared that Seth's habit of pounding on the vestry windows to be let in would break the glass. On one particularly raucous evening as dusk began to settle, the sexton unlocked the door to the vestry and ordered Seth to stop. Going on the offensive worked—the pounding ceased.

Several church members are convinced that Seth's ghost has a low tolerance level for mischievous boys. The tale they share involves the custodian, who was working alone in the kitchen one frigid, snow-bound morning. Three local boys knocked on the lower window. They were cold and asked to be let in and warm up. The custodian unlocked the main doors and allowed them inside. No sooner had the boys thawed out before they began to "hoot and holler" upstairs as they ran back and forth between the pews. Then, the custodian heard them "clattering down one side of the curving staircase in the vestibule and slamming the front door shut." A few minutes later, the icy chill drove the boys back to the warmth of the church. Once again, with frozen fingers they tapped at the vestry window. Peeved by their behavior but taking pity, the custodian opened the doors a second time but insisted on knowing why they went back outside. The boys glanced furtively from one to the other, unsure if they should tell, until the tallest among them stepped forward and mumbled, "We were scared. A man jumped out from behind the pulpit and chased us." A second boy piped up, "He didn't want us there." The custodian knew there was no man upstairs in the sanctuary. The young culprits had had a run-in with Seth, who did not "abide by boys getting into deviltry."

Mary Beth Splaine is the president of the South Church Preservation Fund, a non-profit group formed to raise funds to

The ghost of Seth jumped out from behind the pulpit, scaring the boys away.

maintain and preserve the historic church building. She has listened to numerous Seth stories and attributes them to "old wives tales." The tall, elegantly dressed president is not judgmental; she simply believes that the stories remain in circulation because ghost tours bring people to South Church and regale them with accounts of Seth running around inside.

At a reception after one Sunday's service, Susan Jarrell, the music director of the late 1970s through the early 1980s, shared her belief that Seth is not the only ghost who enters unannounced. "I was sitting at the organ practicing one Sunday morning before service, and two soldiers marched in wearing Revolutionary War garb—red pants, swords, black hats." Jarrell remembers that she was startled but "just went back to practicing and they left." Even though Ted Anderson, the minister at the time, "did not believe in any of this stuff," Jarrell, now a woman in her eighties, did not back down. "I just report the facts." A petite figure in a royal purple jacket, Jarrell whispers conspiratorially that there are many haunted accounts about Seth. His ghost has been here long before she was a member.

In the lower level of the church, there is a large, framed needlepoint hanging on the back wall. Embroidered on it is the roll call of ministers. "SETH F. SWIFT" appears as number one. In 1810, the proprietors (the voting members, those who gave money to erect the church) asked twenty-one-year-old Seth Freeman Swift to be their first minister. Seth was a Cape Cod native who came to Nantucket to teach. In order to gain the acceptance and respect of his new congregation, bachelor Seth had to marry—the original proprietors insisted that before becoming the spiritual counselor to their wives and daughters, he must first find himself a wife. Fortuitously for Seth, Valina Rawson already had the minister-to-be in her sights. They wed and went on to produce a proper brood of four: Caroline, Edward, Joseph, and Charles, though the youngest never made it to his first birthday.

Fresh out of Harvard, the idealistic young minister initiated a lending library and a commitment to race-blind justice, radical innovations back in 1810. Based on oral history accounts, Swift was

The needlepoint wall hanging with the list of the early ministers.

held in high esteem by the small free-black community that lived in a section of Nantucket called New Guinea, many members of which had arrived on the island as slaves. In particular, Seth officiated at their weddings, including several of the family of Capt. Absalom Boston, the commander of the *Industry,* a whaling vessel that sailed with an all-black crew in 1822.

Minister Swift's typical sermons before his congregation lasted more than an hour and averaged thirty-two pages in length. Biblical passages were quoted in full, not merely cited by chapter and verse. For those sitting in the pews, these mind-numbing sermons must have felt interminable, and the large clock inside the sanctuary strategically placed to face the pulpit did little to prod the long-winded minister to wrap things up. The inscription on the clock is *Tempus Fugit* (time flies). In an article for the church's two-hundredth anniversary, minister emeritus Reverend Anderson refers to a young lad who inadvertently mistranslated the phrase—but perhaps more

Tempus Fugit, *on the clock below the choir loft.*

accurately captured the perspective of the attendees. He translated this inscription as "Time Fidgets."

Rev. Seth Swift held many liberal views yet was a stickler for lengthy dissertations and lectures to his parishioners, requiring proper conduct in church and at home. On March 1, 1815, a committee was appointed to review the behavior of a "sister" in the congregation who had used "vulgar language" and showed no signs of "humility or penitence." For this offence and for her general improper conduct, including "tale bearing," the sister was "suspended from communion with the church indefinitely." Several more members were excommunicated for "intemperance," "breach of morality," and "falsehood." When current practices in the church deviate from those of Seth's, his ever-rigid spirit engages in some heavy-duty poltergeist activity.

A trustee of the South Church Preservation Fund, Craig Spery is very familiar with any "questionable mishaps." Spery points the finger squarely at their ghost: "Seth did it."

From its founding, South Church functioned as an integral part of community life: a meeting hall for civic and social activities, command central for the "Fire Watch," the keeper of island time through the clock tower and belfry, and a navigational aid. In a January 1965 article for *Historic Nantucket*, H. Errol Coffin describes the tower as "completely functional from grade to weather vane." The original tower, which rises over the double front doors, had to be rebuilt in 1827, as the great Portuguese bell had weakened the structure by striking not only the hours (156 times a day) but also the "52s," struck after the hours of 7 a.m., noon, and the 9 p.m. curfew—an additional 156 times. The new tower, completed in 1833, is capped by a golden dome and is 109 feet, 5 1/2" inches, above the sidewalk.

The first town clock was installed on the tower in 1823. However, certain mischief needed to be addressed. According to the local paper:

> August 5, 1823. Town Clock. The publick are hereby informed why this instrument is so frequently out of order, that there may be no blame attached to the workmanship of the machinery, or to its being stopped from striking during the nights or to the carelessness of the superintendent.
>
> The cause is this: Boys have had too free access to the tower and have frequently entangled the hands at the dials. The proprietors of the Meeting House are determined there shall be no more public keys to the tower for the future.
>
> Those persons therefore who wish to view the clock machinery are informed that an opportunity occurs every Saturday afternoon after 4 o'clock, at which time it is wound up.
>
> R. W. Jenks, Supt.

The first town clock on the tower ticked admirably (minus a slight interruption by a few young rascals) until it was replaced in 1881, a gift to the town by William Hadwen Starbuck. The clock was run by weights from May 28, 1881, until it was electrified in 1957.

While Nantucket residents look with pride to the town clock, the ghost of the Reverend Swift brooded over the childish antics and the

The clock tower and belfry of South Church.

changes. The recent additions of a cell phone tower and a web camera were unacceptable to the church's first minister, and he signaled his displeasure by blocking access to all levels of the tower.

South Church trustee Craig Spery feels that it is time for Seth to step aside and understand that he is no longer in charge. Dressed in a crisp blue shirt and tan slacks, Spery leads a tour up multiple narrow stairwells, each at tight right angles to the next. The first landing is level with the choir loft; the next is the watchman's level. Much of the aged wood has deepened from brown to charcoal black. A chain-link fence protects the mechanicals (heating, electrical, alarm systems) from curious hands. The need for protection is obvious. Every square inch of the walls, including the underside of the stair steps, is covered in graffiti; names and dates have been carved into the wood with pocket knives and scrawled in chalk, ink, pencil, and paint. For more than two centuries, workmen, repairmen, staff, and visitors all have felt compelled to sign their names. Some of

Early graffiti in the watchtower room.

the earliest graffiti dates to 1876, 1894, and 1912. A few contemporary jokesters tried to leave the impression that both Chuck Norris and Elvis also paid tribute by signing in.

Other than its appeal as an irresistible canvas, the room served an important purpose. "You can still see the wainscoting and plaster walls," says Spery. "There was a potbelly stove with a chimney behind it, so the watchmen and the bell ringers would be able to stay in this room. The rope for the bell tower came down to this floor, and every hour they would ring the bell." After the Great Nantucket Fire in 1846, two fire watchmen were also stationed here. They took turns: one hour on duty, one hour off.

The tower was a busy place. In 1849, the postman and town crier were given keys. Billy Clark (1846-1909) was the best known town crier. He stood out in any crowd. With his top hat and distinct long neck, he appeared "nearly seven feet tall." Clark rang his large brass bell and announced the daily news with a "fish-horn voice." He also climbed the South Church tower every morning to get the first glimpse of the steamer carrying mail. On sighting the steamer, he would thrust his tin horn through the slots of the belfry and sound it in all four directions. In addition to his other duties, Clark made the steep climb during heavy storms to watch for shipwrecks or distressed boats. During inclement weather, in the lull between the peals of the bell in the belfry, people hurrying by swear they still hear the toot of Billy Clark's tin horn.

Each level of the tower holds its secrets. The level above the watchmen's purview provides access to the clock. Spery removes a small block cut into the wall above the clock face. Approximately five by seven inches, the hole is just large enough for a hand to reach through to pull in the spotlight mounted on a swinging arm and change the bulb. There is a magnificent view of Nantucket harbor. The final staircase leads to the belfry and the original Portuguese bronze bell, which still chimes.

With the tour at its conclusion, Spery reveals why he is so annoyed with Seth. Standing at some six-feet-plus in height, he steps over to a graffiti-covered panel that is about another foot above his head.

"I came up here to check on a new installation by Verizon, and I couldn't open the door to the room on the first level. This panel had fallen and wedged the door shut." An exasperated Spery exhales audibly and rubs his hand over his neatly trimmed beard. "Now, that shouldn't happen. No air from the outside gets in here—no gust of wind knocked it over. No ladder from the outside could have reached this level. That panel is from the shaft which had the weights from the clock and now houses cables and wires for the cell towers." Spery says they had to find a stick, slide it under the door, and slowly maneuver the heavy wooden panel out of the way. After finally being able to access the room, they secured the panel back in place. Spery called out, "Okay, Seth, that's enough." But it wasn't.

Within a few months of the first incident, Seth blocked the entrance to the choir loft. At the top of the right side of the double staircase in the vestibule is a narrow door. Spery explains that they had stored a spare pew door on the landing that leads to the choir loft. To raise funds to build the original church, pews were sold and owned by individual families. Each pew has a numbered half-door. Occasionally, a pew door gets broken off its hinges or needs repairs, and the trustees like to keep a spare handy as a quick replacement. "Yeah," says Spery, "Seth was at it again. Maybe he didn't approve of one of the hymns, but when I tried to open the door to the choir loft it wouldn't budge. The pew door, which had been up against the wall, was now lying on its side; it basically locked this door." There was no easy solution.

"We couldn't take the hinges off because they were on the inside. My brother-in-law came up with the idea of tying a string to a screw, getting the screw into the edge of the pew door from underneath, and then working the string around inch-by-inch until we could lift the pew door from the outside." Extra pew doors are no longer stored inside the stairwell to the choir loft. Spery drops his arms in exasperation; they slap against his hips. "This happened, like, within two months of the tower door being blocked. It was a little more than a coincidence. I'm like, 'Come on, Seth!'"

Unitarians are a forgiving lot. Their services are open to all interested parties. The ghost of Seth Swift might do well to loosen his tight collar and enjoy the camaraderie and fellowship instead of working so hard to keep everyone in line.

Lagniappe: What's in a name? In the beginning, there were two Congregational Society churches on the island: the "first" and the "second" congregations. At the start of the nineteenth century, the population of Nantucket was booming. Congregationalism was the state-sanctioned religion in the Puritan tradition of New England Calvinism. The Second Congregational Meeting House was incorporated in 1809 by an act of the Massachusetts legislature. Built on the south side of Main Street, it became known by all as the South Church. In 1837, the congregation of the South Church adopted the Harvard Covenant, becoming Unitarian. In the same year, the Universalist church on Nantucket disbanded and sold its building. Some of its members joined South Church. In 1961, the two denominations merged, and South Church officially became Unitarian Universalist. It is a mouthful, but as the new plaque on the front of the building states, the official name of the church that Seth haunts on Orange Street in Nantucket is the Second Congregational Meeting House Society, Unitarian Universalist.

Highfield Hall in Beebe Woods.

2

A Tangled Tale

High in the wooded hills above Falmouth, two brothers built two mammoth mansions: Highfield Hall and Tanglewood. One mansion lives on, while the saga of the souls of the lost mansion has migrated to the structure still standing. Tracking the origins of any good ghost story is much like an archeological dig—each fragmented artifact or bone must be carefully dusted off and held to the light to discern where it fits.

Popular local legend holds that the ghost of Highfield Hall is Emily Beebe. Her heels make tiny clicking sounds as she descends the main staircase from her second-floor bedroom to the wide central hallway. The phantom Emily is on her way to join brother Arthur and his wife for a glittering dinner party at their Tanglewood estate. Alas, poor Emily gets lost in the woods because her brother's home has vanished. The confused spirit wanders aimlessly until she finds the path back to Highfield, where she is doomed to repeat her nocturnal journey over and over.

Besieged by requests from various ghost-hunting groups to communicate with the spirit—or spirits—of Highfield Hall, the non-profit board that manages the historic property originally refused. "We did forbid it for a long time, but in 2012 we relented," says a resigned Barbara J. Milligan, CEO and president of Highfield Hall and Gardens. "Last year, we said, yes—let's just get it over with." The reversal of the no-ghost-hunting policy came about because the board felt that an additional source of revenue would be helpful. "We opened ourselves up to the possibilities that maybe there was something we could use for an entertaining tour." Milligan

Emily's ghost reputedly walks down the staircase at Highfield Hall.

avoids identifying the paranormal group that was allowed to conduct the investigation. "They came in and made a presentation to us afterwards. They told us, 'We definitely found entities,' or whatever they call it." There is a tinge of regret in Milligan's voice as she relates the conclusion of the investigation. "They had to work very hard to show us anything. They played a digital recording back for us and they say it's a voice, an EVP [Electronic Voice Phenomenon]." After listening to the recording several times, Milligan told the investigators that the EVP "sounds like a member of your team." The investigators then produced images of orbs. Many parapsychologists define orbs as balls of energy or light that are the remnants of the deceased, much like fingerprints left behind. Milligan asked the paranormal team whose spirit they thought they had found. "They told us, 'We believe this is Emily because she died here.' And I'm like, 'No, she didn't.'"

The knowledgeable executive in her fitted lime-green jacket rolls blue eyes beneath a halo of pale blonde waves. She is aware that this group, like so many others, has identified the wrong Emily. "She is probably talked about the most because she lived the longest, so she is part of the story, but Emily Beebe of Highfield Hall lived until she was almost eighty and died in Boston." Both Milligan and Highfield Hall's board of directors abandoned the idea of a haunted tour of the historic home. "We thought if there is anything . . . to these ghost stories, let's just use it to make money. That is one of the reasons we brought this paranormal group in . . . but there was not enough to hang any program on."

Yet, there was more than one Emily in the family, and the true Beebe family history is rife with depression, mental illness, shootings, and suicides. The two family mansions, Highfield Hall and Tanglewood, suffered from neglect, abandonment, lawsuits—and in the case of Tanglewood, total demolition. Reports of hauntings, apparitions, and paranormal activities flourished from the time the last Beebe left the premises in 1932.

With the arrival of the railroad in Falmouth in 1872, the small farming and fishing community emerged as a prime summer destination for residents of sweltering cities such as Boston and

J. Arthur Beebe's Tanglewood mansion, prior to demolition.

New York. Wealthy manufacturing czar James Madison Beebe was among the first to see the town's potential. James and his wife, Esther, purchased a summer home they called Vineyard Lodge on Shore Street. With an eye for future expansion, James Beebe also purchased seven hundred acres of prime hill land above the railroad station.

Shortly after their father's death in 1875, two of his sons built grand residences on the hill that would be known as Beebe Woods. In 1878, Pierson Beebe, along with another brother, Frank, and their sister Emily moved into Highfield Hall. A year later, brother J. Arthur Beebe oversaw the construction of an adjacent mansion, Tanglewood, a little farther uphill.

When the paranormal group identified Emily as the ghost of Highfield Hall, they may have had the right name but referred to the wrong girl at the wrong house. For a time, there were three Emilys in the Beebe family all living on the conjoined estates of Highfield Hall and Tanglewood.

*The haunted Beebe family. Top row: Emily Appleton. Next row: J. Arthur
Beebe, with a straw hat; his daughter, Emily Esther; Pierson, with a boutonniere;
and a bearded Frank. Next row: The first Emily. Bottom row: Young Arthur
Appleton, in a white cap and knickers; Charles Philip; and Mary Louisa, with
a parasol.*

James Madison Beebe's progeny, seven in all, were Emily Brown, Mary Louisa, Charles Edwin, Edward Pierson, James Arthur, and Franklin (Frank). Also a part of the enclave were J. Arthur's wife, Emily Appleton, and their children: Arthur Appleton (eldest), Charles Philip (youngest), and, in between her brothers, Emily Esther, named for her mother and grandmother.

Along with a large contingent of house servants, gardeners, and assorted staff, Beebe Woods bustled with activity. Frequent visitors and house guests swelled these numbers so that Highfield Hall and Tanglewood appeared as a village unto itself.

Siblings Pierson, Frank, and socialite sister Emily never married. They split their time between their Boston townhomes and Highfield Hall in Falmouth. They threw lavish parties, traveled extensively in Europe, and enjoyed the finest life had to offer.

For other family members, life was not as kind. Oldest brother Charles died unexpectedly while traveling in France in 1866; he was only twenty-seven. Mary Louisa died of a rare form of cancer in 1883. Fannie, the only sister to marry, lost her husband just two years after their 1866 wedding. Fannie became a single mother to two toddlers.

For J. Arthur and his wife, Emily Appleton Beebe, life unraveled quickly. Death, like an insidious monster, grabbed them in its talons and would not let go. In 1900, their twenty-eight-year-old son committed suicide. Young Arthur Appleton graduated from Harvard Medical School and was completing a residency at Massachusetts General Hospital when he walked into his room at the family home in Boston and shot himself.

Son Arthur's death almost seemed preordained. In July of 1893, seven years prior, a flurry of newspapers erroneously reported that J. Arthur Beebe's son had drowned in a boating accident. Young Arthur was sailing that day on his boat, the *Nobska,* and took first place in the regatta. A fellow competitor, Henry Bellows, was the actual drowning victim. The *Boston Globe* later published a correction under the headline "Arthur Beebe Not Drowned," but the shock of the false report may have caused irreparable damage. When Arthur

chose to end his life with a bullet, his mother, Emily Appleton
Beebe, and his sister, Emily Esther, did not attend his funeral, as
both were said to suffer from a nervous condition. Rumors persisted
in Falmouth that there was a "taint" in the Appleton blood. Emily
Appleton Beebe was remembered as "a very quiet person who was
deeply depressed." The inconsolable mother died in 1911.

Having lost one child to suicide, and perhaps to avert any future
repercussions, J. Arthur packed up his distraught daughter for a
series of lengthy trips abroad. Eerily, in 1912, another false news
report preceded their deaths. The premature announcement, if it
had come to pass, would have doomed the pair: "J. Arthur Beebe
and daughter Emily are booked to return from Europe on the new
liner, Titanic." The father-daughter duo missed the ill-fated ship, yet
death was not averted.

Less than a year later, Emily chose to copy her brother. She
entered a room at the Hotel Touraine in Boston, locked the door,
pulled out a revolver, and shot herself in the chest. When the news
reached J. Arthur, he ordered his chauffeur to race to his daughter's
side. In his haste, the chauffeur struck and killed ten-year-old Henry
Sombaulski, who was crossing the road. The newspapers vilified the
chauffeur, Arthur, and Emily: "Society Girl Imitated Her Brother's
Little Suicide Stunt." They implied that if Arthur's spoiled debutante
daughter hadn't gone "the gun route," an innocent boy would have
still been alive.

The haunting of the J. Arthur Beebe family was nearly complete.
J. Arthur died of heart failure on November 28, 1914. His one
surviving son, Charles Philip, then succumbed to the mental illness
that plagued his family. He was in and out of mental institutions and
lived out the remainder of his life on his farm, always accompanied
by a male attendant from McLean Hospital. On May 20, 1977,
Tanglewood, their once magnificent family mansion, was leveled by
a wrecker's ball.

There is a widely held belief that the souls or spirits of the dead
cling to their former homes when tragedy is involved. Barbara
Milligan would like to dispel the misconceptions. "Nobody died

here [at Highfield Hall], not a single one of them. That's why it is so frustrating." Milligan does acknowledge that the historic home she oversees barely avoided the same fate as Tanglewood. "After the Beebes died, it went through a series of abuses." Highfield Hall sat abandoned and deteriorating for two decades, the subject of lawsuits and ghost tales.

When Frank Beebe, the last of the Beebe siblings, died in 1932, the trust that administered the family fortune put the estate on the market. In his epic 1976 narrative *Ring Around the Punch Bowl,* author George Moses writes, "The ghosts of the Beebes, the greatest hosts the town has ever known, lingered on at Highfield."

Tanglewood had a similar reputation as a family haunt. After the deaths of his wife and son, J. Arthur Beebe showed little interest in the mansion; it fell into decline. In a newspaper article, Moses paints a scene of Gothic ruins. "It towers above its satellite buildings—one time stables and two cottages . . . like a bedraggled old beldame looking disdainfully down at lesser beings." In his will, Arthur bequeathed his Tanglewood estate to Harvard University. Harvard put Tanglewood up for sale. With no immediate takers, it was leased to summer renters. Moses Sloat Fassett Hodgson remembers staying with his well-to-do grandmother Jennie Crocker Fassett at Tanglewood and dealing with the resident ghost. "Doors in the place had a habit of opening all by themselves. When this occurred . . . it was the custom to say, politely, 'Come in, Mr. Beebe.'"

Now, there are no doors to open or hallways for any ghost to roam. The "joyful jumble" of Tanglewood's main manor house, with its numerous porches, dormers, and gables adorned with gingerbread, was demolished down to the last timber frame. A drive through the woods along the paved pathway to the semi-circle drive reveals only the precarious remnants of J. Arthur's Beebe's grand dream. Tanglewood's stable and two cottages are the sole holdouts, and they too seem on the verge of self-imploding.

If there are any hauntings attributed to Tanglewood, it would most likely be the ghost of Philip, the troubled youngest son of J. Arthur and Emily Appleton Beebe. As a child, Charles Philip was

An empty field is all that remains of the once-magnificent Tanglewood.

Tanglewood stables, one of three service buildings left on the estate.

regarded as far from normal. Charlotte Nickerson, the daughter of Tanglewood's superintendent, recalls that Philip spent much of his time in the estate's workshop puttering with tools—an unusual "lower-class" hobby for the son of the estate's master. "He did seem odd—peculiar—to us kids." There remains a functioning workshop housed in one of remaining service buildings. Whether Philip's spirit hangs out there is a matter of conjecture, one that any paranormal investigator would be eager to resolve.

In 1952, new owner DeWitt TerHeun remodeled Highfield. Using a picture of a Southern colonial mansion as a guide, TerHeun ordered the Falmouth contractor to replace the Beebes' English country façade with six white pillars supporting an open, two-story portico. This dramatic makeover into a faux Southern plantation home is how people of recent generations remember Highfield. Following TerHeun's death in 1962, the estate passed through several owners. Later, in the 1980s and well into the 1990s as it sat vacant, vandals and vagrants wreaked havoc on the grounds. Delicate Delft tiles were broken off the parlor's fireplace, and graffiti marred the walls. Lights flashed on and off at odd hours. In 1993, a Falmouth police officer complained that the derelict mansion was monitored by a shoddy alarm system that "went off every time a raccoon entered the house." Its reputation grew as "the spooky plantation house on the hill," where "phantom music played." The abandoned 17,800-square-foot house, with its 157 windows (10 of stained glass), 84 doors, and 15 fireplaces (each with a different mantel), left the accounting of ghostly inhabitants open-ended.

At Highfield Hall, visitors in 2001, arriving for the first time since its rescue and restoration, felt like someone was playing tricks. The white-pillared plantation house of their memories was nowhere to be found. The haunted house on the hill had been restored to the buff-colored Queen Anne grand dame of the Beebe family.

The CEO of Highfield House and Gardens offers a theory for the proliferation of ghost sightings—a female apparition that hovers over the staircase, a woman in a long brown dress scurrying down a hallway, the presence of an elderly man on the third floor—to the

Highfield Hall, remodeled into a Southern plantation home in the 1950s.

conditions of the then-barely surviving Beebe mansion. It had been in use as dormitories and storage space for the theatre operating in the old barn. "The house was boarded up. The ceiling was falling in." Barbara Milligan waves her hand in the direction of the front section of the house. "This room was full of theatre costumes and dresses. That room was full of wigs. Teenagers were sneaking in and out, you know, the way they do, so kids are going to come up with stories, 'This is the haunted house,' and telling tales to scare each other." Milligan doesn't know why they picked on Emily as the main ghost in residence. "I don't know how that happened."

If it is not Emily Brown Beebe's spirit who descends the stairs at Highfield to visit her brother J. Arthur at Tanglewood, then there is an alternate spin to this haunted saga: niece Emily is equally lost; the disturbed woman who took her own life cannot return to her cherished childhood home. Tanglewood is gone, but the elegantly restored Highfield Hall, home to her aunt and uncles, is alive with music and celebrations, much as it was when she was a little girl. Here, young Emily's spirit can peer over the rails of the upper landing and watch today's well-dressed guests dance to live music at the annual Holiday Ball.

While the term "haunted house" most often carries a negative connotation, the application to a historic site can simply mean that the previous occupants have left their imprint, cemented themselves as part of its history. The Beebe family, through their triumphs and their tragedies, created a baronial lifestyle that changed the face of Falmouth.

Lagniappe: Highfield Hall has reclaimed its status as the cultural center of Falmouth. Art exhibitions, concerts, lectures, culinary programs, and nature walks are available to the community. Holidays at Highfield Hall are highly anticipated events. The private house survived many adapted uses as a health resort, sanatorium, religious retreat, hotel, and dormitory for aspiring thespians, and it even managed to escape a developer's proposal to be carved up into five hundred residential lots. Rescued by Mr. and Mrs. Josiah K. Lilly III, Highfield Hall lasted through a protracted seven-year lawsuit until it was seized through eminent domain by the town of Falmouth and restored to as it was during the golden era of the Beebes by determined citizen activists. The front room of Highfield Hall houses a permanent exhibit, *The Highfield Story*. A large panel features a series of miniature wooden doors with frequently asked questions. Flip the door open, and the answer is revealed. The last question and answer is the most popular: "How many ghosts?" The answer: "You decide."

3

Cue Faye

Be hole, be dust, be dream, be wind.
Be night, be dark, be wish, be mind.
Now slip, now slide, now move unseen.
Above, beneath, betwixt, between.
—Neil Gaiman, *The Graveyard Book*

Curtains swish open. Lights dim for ambiance. Sets create illusions. Costumed characters prance, stomp, and waltz across the stage. Voices reverberate in the cavernous space. And, like every reputable theatre around the globe, at least one ghost lurks in the wings. At Highfield Theatre in Falmouth, the lead female on the playbill is Faye.

When there is no performance and the curtains are closed, Faye plays with the seats. She slams them open in a rapid staccato succession. A member of the theatre troupe arrives early for rehearsals. The banging is alarming. The frightened stage manager flips on the lights, but a check reveals that all the seats are in their proper upright positions. Faye has never been caught in the act.

Faye is fond of music—piano music. Her phantom fingers skim the keys; she is partial to raucous notes rather than the theatre's favored light fare of Gilbert and Sullivan ditties.

Highfield's ghost ignores the energy-efficient guidelines. A darkened backstage area ignites her repertoire of ghostly pranks. Staff and volunteers turn the lights off as they exit the prop and dressing rooms; Faye follows behind and clicks them back on.

Faye likes make-up. She absconds with lipsticks, brushes, and eyeliners and then randomly scatters them in hallways.

Occasionally, Faye opts for a personal appearance. She has

materialized before a startled set designer toiling alone on a portrait for an upcoming production. He wasn't bothered by her period costume or her announcement that she "used to live here." It was her disappearing act that made his jaw drop—she didn't exit stage left or stage right but morphed into a misty form and vanished.

Theatre guild members are left to speculate who she is and why the Highfield Theatre is her haunt of choice. Her announcement that she "used to live here" has led to more than one local legend.

During the heyday of Highfield Hall, owners Pierson, Emily, and Frank Beebe hosted many scintillating soirees. Famous singers, musicians, and theatrical personalities gave private performances for the Beebe siblings and their socially prominent guests. Frank was a well-known patron of the arts both in Boston and at his summer residence in Falmouth. In 1932, the University Players gave evening performances at the Old Silver Beach theatre in West Falmouth. Although he favored plays, Frank, then in his eighties, did not like to go out at night. He struck a deal: if the players would agree to a weekly midday performance, he would personally pay for ten season subscriptions. The Wednesday matinee was born.

The Old Silver Beach theatre burned to the ground on Labor Day eve of 1936. Summer theatre in Falmouth lay dormant for the next eleven years. In 1947, the *Falmouth Enterprise* announced that New York and Hollywood producer Arthur Beckhard had purchased the former Beebe estates of Highfield and neighboring Tanglewood to be the home of a professional summer troupe. The manor houses would be used as hotels for guests, and Highfield's large barn repurposed as the Tanglewood Theatre.

The refurbishing required some ingenious alterations. George Moses, in *Ring Around the Punch Bowl,* gives a rundown of a few of the novel renovations: sloping the barn floor to the level of the manure pit to create inclined seating, raising the main stall for the stage, and fashioning dressing rooms out of the remaining horse stalls. The carriage room was transformed into a cocktail lounge, and props were stored in the harness room. Although today's theatre patrons might find the theatre's rustic origins charming, they might be a tad unnerved to learn that they have just parked their cars over the graves of family pets.

Highfield Theatre, after its conversion from the barn.

To make room for a two-hundred-car parking lot, part of the old Beebe pet cemetery was plowed under. The 1887 death of Elcho, the cherished family dog, prompted the distressed Beebes to found a pet cemetery, complete with inscribed markers and monuments, in close proximity to the main house. The news of such "odd behavior" only confirmed the local gossip that there was a very eccentric family in their midst.

The revelation by Highfield's long-time caretaker that, at each interment, the dogs were buried in lined caskets and the servants were recruited to serve as pallbearers caused eyebrows to ratchet up another notch. The disposal of these same caskets, monuments, and grave markers remains in question. For those who believe that the spirits of pets, like their human owners, can come back to haunt former stomping grounds, it did not make for an auspicious start to the theatrical enterprise.

Producer Arthur J. Beckhard's intent to make his new theatre "an incubator of talent and a source of new plays on Broadway" was greatly hampered by his poor finances. Foreclosure proceedings were filed, but an angel arrived in the guise of theatre-lover DeWitt TerHeun and his wife, Clare. The *Falmouth Enterprise* had high praise for the new estate owners and their deep pockets. "The ghosts of the Beebes must be applauding."

Attendance at the renamed Highfield Theatre increased. Under TerHeun's watchful supervision, the third floor of Highfield Hall housed the young males of the new resident company of twenty-four college students, while the young women were sequestered at nearby Tanglewood. Moses writes that the separate dormitories ensured that whatever the young actors did after hours, "They didn't do it under the old roofs of Highfield and Tanglewood amid the ghosts of bachelor brothers and maiden sisters," referring to the Beebe siblings, who never married during their tenure at Highfield.

The repeated mention of ghosts in newspaper articles, books, and local lore adds fuel to the haunted status of Highfield Theatre. Ghost-in-residence Faye has had a long run. There are as many versions of her true identity as there are characters in a Shakespearean tragedy.

A paranormal internet blog infers that illusive Faye might be "the girl who killed herself on the second floor of the mansion, and you can see her ghost there." Barbara Milligan, CEO and president of historic Highfield Hall and Gardens, responds, "We searched the newspaper accounts and we could find no reports on that." Milligan is equally unimpressed with similar claims. "I have heard Faye was a member of the Beebe family. There was never a Faye in the Beebe family."

With little regard for the facts, fanciful accounts persist: Faye fell in love with a stable hand, and when the family found out, they fired the boy and Faye killed herself—death by hanging, presumably in the barn (now the theatre), where the lovers had their trysts. Milligan says she has even heard that Faye, in a role reversal, was a servant. "No one named Faye was a servant at Highfield. Then I heard she was a lover of a servant. None of the children of the servants that we still have connections with recalls anyone named Faye associated with their families."

Actors are a superstitious lot. "Break a leg" is a sincere good luck phrase, not a curse. Rituals and lucky charms are a necessary means of getting through a performance. A resident ghost is a convenient catch-all to absorb the inexplicable—missing make-up, loud bangs, flickering lights, a sudden, cold draft—cue Faye!

A few of the more inventive actors say Faye dwells in the woods. A mischievous sprite? A fairy? A wood nymph? Beebe Woods forms a tight perimeter around the theater complex, and stories about the woods are whoppers: blood-curdling yells, screams of "Help me! Help me," and a band of monks unable to find their way out. Surprisingly, there is documentation to prove the latter true.

In the summer of 1890, Father Ignatius, a rebellious fifty-three-year-old monk of the Church of England, led his followers from Llanthony Abbey in Wales to Falmouth. They arrived via an invitation from the "Duchess of Tanglewood," Emily Appleton Beebe, wife of J. Arthur, the owner of Tanglewood manor in Beebe Woods. The

The entrance to the haunted Beebe Woods.

"Duchess" met the charismatic monk during a return voyage from France. Father Ignatius wove his spell, and the enchanted Emily paid for his accommodations in Cape Cod. The book *Father Ignatius in America* recounts his many adventures, including a disastrous visit to Beebe Woods, then encompassing some seven hundred acres of dense forestland. Led by three local children, the monk and his followers set out in the morning to find the Punch Bowl, a kettle pond hidden in a deep ravine. When the explorers and their youthful guides didn't return for their evening repast, church bells tolled and search parties began to scour the woods. Nine harrowing hours after their disappearance, the lost souls were rescued from their terrifying ordeal. The monks made it out alive, but another less fortunate explorer didn't.

Frank N. Whitman was addicted to long, solitary hikes from Woods Hole to Falmouth through Beebe Woods. Late in the winter of 1962, seventy-six-year-old Frank took off and never returned. The well-known ornithologist and author of *Familiar Studies of Wild Birds* had known every inch of the woods from the time he was a child. Frank's disappearance sparked the most massive search ever conducted in the woods since the Welsh monks had lost their way. Helicopters directed the ground search by police, game wardens, and Boy Scouts. The woods were still recovering from the great fire of 1947, so underbrush was not an issue and visibility was good. Still, no Frank was found.

In 1972, an unfortunate hiker stumbled across some scattered human bones. A positive identification could not be made, but several coins in the vicinity of the remains bore dates up to, but not beyond, 1961. Beebe Woods gave up Frank Whitman's bones, but the mystery surrounding his death was never solved.

For the Beebes and successive owners, protecting their sacred woods from "outsiders" was a battle. These "invaders" ran the gamut: game poachers; blueberry, blackberry, and huckleberry scavengers; Mayflower pickers; drag-racing dare devils; pot-smoking hippies; indiscreet teenage lovers; and ghost hunters. One volunteer who worked on the restoration of Highfield's buildings and walked in the woods is ambivalent about the haunted rumors. "I suppose anyone could find the woods creepy. The noises might be the large population of coyotes that inhabit the woods or the fact the woods are a popular place for underage drinking and partying." The volunteer qualifies his statement: "I do not dispute the fact that the woods may be haunted."

High-pitched screams and ear-splitting yells have emanated from the ravine as local kids dared each other to fling themselves off a rope swing into the bottomless pit of the Punch Bowl. Backfire from the exhaust of early cars roaring along the old carriage trails has reverberated like the deafening retort of gunshots at close range. Hazy female forms have floated through the thicket of one patch of trees. All of these have inspired multiple "Fayes."

According to present-day members of the Falmouth Theatre Guild, their Faye is having way too much fun. The ghost-in-residence shows no sign of taking a final curtain call.

Lagniappe: The Highfield Theatre complex is located directly behind historic Highfield Hall. The College Light Opera Company, or CLOC, performs during the summer season, and the Falmouth Theatre Guild hosts plays and musicals in the fall and winter. Beebe Woods is owned by the town of Falmouth and open to the public as a 383-acre conservation area. The myth of the Punch Bowl's bottomless pit has been refuted by naturalist Robert Finch, whose soundings revealed the average depth to be eleven to fourteen feet. To ensure the enjoyment of the woods, and to protect it from future devastation, the town insists on a few guidelines: no overnight camping, campfires, cutting of wood, hunting, motorized vehicles, or smoking. Ghost hunting is optional.

The John Pope House, formerly the Tupper Inn.

4

The House with
Multiple Personalities

*Houses are not haunted. We are haunted, and regardless of the
architecture with which we surround ourselves, our ghosts stay with us
until we ourselves are ghosts.*
                                              —Dean Koontz, *Velocity*

It's not just the ghosts who keep the evenings lively, but the guests
who accidentally go bump in the night when wandering through the
maze of architectural oddities at the Tupper Inn in Sandwich. Owner
Jana Hamby explains that with so many previous owners tacking
on their own twists and embellishments, "There's not a right angle
in the house . . . the floors slope up, down, weaving and bobbing
every which way." There are also disappearing stairs, doors that lead
nowhere, guillotine windows, and secret panels and passageways. For
a few anxious spirits, the 1699 Colonial home remains a safe haven.

Two years ago, a man driving by the inn spotted a wispy apparition
levitating near the side door. "He stopped, came up to the house,
knocked on the door, and said, 'I saw this pale woman in a white
cap and a tattered gray dress swooping up the lawn. Her feet did not
touch the ground.'" The man reported that the ghostly form ran past
the old hitching post toward the side door.

The tale of the Colonial-era spirit entering the house was not new
to Hamby. "Back in the 1960s, a teenage girl was sleeping in the
Twin Chamber upstairs. She woke up, and a ghost came in. She told
everyone the next day that the ghost had on a white cap and long
dress and sat on the bed staring at her."

Although the sightings were some fifty years apart, Hamby

The ghost of a woman was seen racing past the old hitching posts.

admits it is quite a coincidence that both the startled motorist and the teenager gave matching descriptions of the female spirit. The innkeeper does not believe in ghosts, but her sister does. "My sister reminded me of the old world belief that when a young mother died, she came back to check on her children. My sister thinks that the woman with pale blue eyes in a white cap and gray dress was John Pope's wife, Elizabeth Bourne Pope, who died when her youngest, Mary, was just a child." The Popes were the first family to live in the house.

Some homes are born of necessity, while others are built as glorified showrooms. For owner and builder Seth Pope, the motivating factor was spite. Eager to explore the world, twenty-two-year-old Seth, the son of Plymouth Puritans, left his family home in Dartmouth seeking adventure—and a pretty girl to be his wife. To support himself, he carried household wares in a sack on his back and sold them door to door as he traveled. He arrived in Sandwich in 1670, but the town selectmen had an aversion to strangers and called on the constable to kick him out of town. With winter approaching, the townsmen feared they might have to feed and house what they perceived to be an indigent, lazy youth who flirted with every eligible female. Hamby feels they misjudged young Seth, who had honorable intentions. "My theory is that Seth was courting his future wife Deborah Perry because when they caught up with him and kicked him out of town, he was near the Perry home." When Seth got on the boat to return home, relates Hamby, "He was so embarrassed and angry that he swore he would come back and buy up the town."

Seth Pope, Esquire, lived up to his threat. In 1674, he married Deborah Perry of Sandwich but wouldn't "live in that damn town." Instead, he went on a buying spree. To the governing men's chagrin, the young man they had booted out had risen to become one of the richest men in Massachusetts Bay province. Seth Pope bought the Dexter gristmill and the miller's house at 10 Grove Street in Sandwich, where years later a truly weird event would be recorded, and built a weaving and fulling mill (a water mill to cleanse cloth of impurities).

Prior to buying the miller's house and mills, Seth purchased acreage on a prominent rise of land overlooking the Mill River and salt marsh. There, on Tupper Road in 1699, Seth built a two-story home consisting of five sections, or bays, for his son John and his new wife, Elizabeth Bourne of Sandwich. Elizabeth gave birth to six children but died at home when her youngest child, Mary, was just a toddler. John Pope remarried. He; his second wife, Experience; and their three children continued to reside in the home until John's death in 1725.

True to his vow, Seth never lived in the house on Tupper Road in Sandwich but did retain ownership. An early, unflattering caricature from a Ripley's Believe It or Not! flyer depicts a haggard unkempt man hunched over from the weight of his back sack and leaning on a cane, labeled "Seth Pope." The caption underneath reads: "A peddler of Sandwich, Mass., who was ordered out of town because it was feared he would become a public charge returned 30 years later and bought the entire area."

In 1710, Seth gave the miller's house on Grove Street, (later known as the Dexter-Pope House) to his son Seth Pope Jr. The next owners were a sea captain and his wife. Shortly after the captain left on a year-long voyage, the wife discovered she was pregnant. She gave birth, but the baby died. Determined that her husband would see his child, she put the little body in a large jar and pickled it. While the Pope family had nothing to do with the pickling, the story attached itself to their name.

Little is known about how often—if ever—Seth visited his son John's home, or if Seth's spirit returns.

Up until December of 2013, Jana and her husband, Bix Hamby, lived in and operated the house as the Tupper Inn. When guests asked whether the house was haunted, they shared what they knew of its history while striving to remain neutral on the topic of the supernatural.

The pickled baby was kept at the Dexter-Pope House.

Jana Hamby speaks of an incident when they first inspected the house with another couple. The wife followed her up the back staircase. She sensed someone was following them, stopped, turned, and called out her husband's name to ask whether it was he. However, they could hear her friend's husband, John, conversing with Bix at the other end of the house. Hamby informed her friend that whatever she sensed behind her was not her husband. On learning that the house had been built by Seth Pope, the friend became convinced that Seth Pope's spirit had been on the stairwell. The next day, the same friend said she had a dream where Seth Pope was walking in the marsh and looking back at the house, happy that someone was moving in.

Much like an amusement park's Fun House, plotting a route through this classic New England home and remembering which paths work and which don't is daunting. The center of what is considered Seth's original house actually is built over a pre-1699 one-room foundation under the present keeping room floor. The name of that occupant is lost to time. Following the death of John Pope, his widow, Experience, and the children moved out of the house on Tupper Road.

In 1749, Seth Pope's grandson and namesake sold the house to Joseph Nye Sr. Nye doubled the size of the Pope house by building a two-story addition in front. The new section is not level with the old, and occasionally, the two structures seem to oppose the "marriage." The jarring sounds generated by the oak gunstock posts and chestnut joists rubbing against each other have caused a few concerns. Hamby stands in the tastefully decorated front parlor of Joseph Nye's addition and stares up at the ceiling. "This morning, at about 6:30, I heard a big crack in the bedroom, and I thought, 'Oh, my goodness,' then I realized it was just the floor or the wall settling with the change of temperature."

The most requested room at the Tupper Inn was the second-floor "secret panel" chamber. It is the largest, and as its name implies, there is a hidden space that inspires mystery and intrigue. "They [guests of the inn] have held séances in this room," says Hamby.

"It was the master bedroom of Joseph and Mehitable Bourne Nye."
Joseph Jr. inherited the house from his father, and it is the son's ever-
vigilant presence that ghost hunters find the most intriguing.

"We had a retired couple who said they were up half the night
talking to the ghosts." The husband had an interesting occupation:
"He was a pre-exorcist. He said there were only two hundred and
fifty priests who perform exorcism, and they were very reluctant, so
the priests would call him in. He would interview the person and
decide if they were possessed or just mad." Hamby crosses her arms
over her petite frame. "Yes, it was creepy that he was telling me this,
but he was a nice guy." The pre-exorcist and his wife would not even
consider the possibility that the "voices" they heard might simply have
been the moans and groans of old timbers shifting back and forth.

Hamby walks over to the bedroom fireplace. The entire side wall
is encased in raised wood panels. She slips her fingers beneath the
narrow, bottom panel to the left of the brick hearth, and lifts it off.

The hidden panel is to the left of the fireplace in the Secret Panel Chamber.

Jana Hamby reveals the entrance to the escape route.

"This was used by Joseph Nye, a loyal patriot, as an escape route during the American Revolution. He wanted to make sure he had a way out if the British or Tories came after him." After Joseph's friend and fellow patriot Dr. Freeman was savagely beaten on his return from a false house call, Joseph became slightly paranoid. He feared that the same kind of ambush might happen to him or his family. If his Tory neighbors chased him into his home, Joseph could run up the front staircase into the master bedroom, remove the secret panel, slither down the crawl space next to the chimney, and emerge in the keeping room, where he could then run out the side door, or, he could continue down the crawl space to the cellar, open the bulkhead door, sprint to the dock across the road on the Mill River, untie his boat, and slip away.

As the house changed ownership, the hidden panel and passageway were forgotten. In the 1960s, a boyfriend of the daughter of the Moodys, later owners who used it as a guest house, did a little exploring. The teenager discovered the secret panel, climbed down next to the chimney, and surprised everyone—especially himself— by stepping out of a closet in the keeping room on the first floor. "The family was just shocked that there was a hiding place in there." Hamby is in awe that anyone could manage to wiggle through, considering the extremely constricted space. "My stepson did it. He is tall, but he managed to pop down there and come out below."

Joseph Nye also had a back-up plan. If there was insufficient time to race up the stairs, he could lock himself and his family in the eighteenth-century version of a safe room. "The Nye family called them 'bugaboo rooms.' The lock was on the inside. There's no lock on the outside." Granted, the door was wood and could be battered open, but Joseph slept better knowing he had some options.

An attractive younger couple tuned into the wonders of the digital age to uncover the house's secrets. Using a "ghost finder" app on their tablet device, they claimed to have pinpointed ghosts in the upstairs bedroom and in the keeping room downstairs. They weren't able to further identify the spirits—male or female, Popes or Nyes—yet the enthusiastic ghost hunters came away satisfied that they experienced a paranormal encounter at the Tupper Inn.

The Safe Room under the staircase.

Jana Hamby shines a light inside the bugaboo room.

The door to the bugaboo room can only by locked from the inside.

Neighbors strolling by on a beautiful Cape Cod summer morning have reported seeing a small girl staring out of the upper window, perhaps little Mary Pope, grieving for her mother who died when she was just a child? The identities of fleeting apparitions are perplexing, and the windows of the historic house have their own inherent issues and dangers. The old wavy glass and bubbles create distortions, looking both in and out. When raised, the windows must be propped open with special sticks and "handled with extreme care," or fingers might be sacrificed. "They're guillotine windows. They are dead weight because of the lead glass and wood." The windows are not the only proceed-at-your-own-risk architectural elements of the house.

For all practical purposes, the wooden exterior door on the left side of the house is an optical illusion; clearly visible from the outside, it can't be found on the inside. The Pope family favored this door, as it was on the side closest to the well, to town, and to church. Joseph Nye relied on it as an emergency exit, part of his escape plan. Interior

The side door leads to nowhere.

access should be through the rear door in the dining room. However, when the door is unlatched, there is a walled-in closet with no exit door.

A peek inside the closet reveals another puzzle. On the right, a short flight of four steep steps disappear into the opposite wall. Hamby searches for an explanation. "I guess someone decided that the steps were too narrow to be functional, and they walled it all off." She accepts this simple rationale, but the inaccessibility of the side door is a constant irritant. When viewed from the outside, the upper half of the wooden door has a glass panel covered by a lace curtain. "It's got this moldering curtain in there that I can't get at that I'd love to get rid of." To reach the offending curtain from the inside, she would have to destroy a wall. No one has a clue when the door was last opened from the outside, as the key is lost.

On the second floor, the jumble of rooms, doors, and walls continues. Midway along a dark, wood-paneled hallway, a doorway

A female entity hovers over the bed in the Twin Chamber.

to the attic is disguised behind a matching panel. Across the narrow hallway in the Twin Chamber favored by the female ghost, there is a raised platform two feet high, which fills a small alcove underneath a window. A rocking chair sits on the platform. "We don't know why that platform is here. It is odd. The people that lived here up until 1971, one of the guys came and said his old aunt used to sit here— her own private watchtower. You could look out at the farm . . . animals would have been up on the top of the hill grazing, and down there on the left is where the stables were." Yet, it seems implausible that an elderly woman would want to heave herself up and over a two-foot-tall platform to reach her rocking chair just for the view.

Hamby's eyes stray to the antique blue coverlets on the pair of matching single beds. "I think this room was originally a children's room." Elizabeth Pope or Experience Pope would have spent their evenings here tucking the children into bed. It is more comforting to picture the spirit of either of these devoted mothers still hovering by the beds, rather than running up the hill over and over again to reunite with their children.

In 1913, the larger bedrooms were subdivided into ten tiny bedrooms when the house became an inn. Walls have been moved so often that only those who have done their homework, such as present owners Jana and Bix Hamby, can detect what went where. The Hambys have also made changes to the Tupper Inn. To start, they added bathrooms. "We didn't want to be carrying chamber pots up and down stairs." And, they created another removable wall on hinges in the Secret Panel Chamber. "My husband built it so the panel can open for families who want to have direct access to the other bedrooms."

The Popes, the Nyes, the Moodys, the Hambys, and their guests have all appreciated their time in the Tupper Inn, and the anxious souls who once lived there know they will always find sanctuary inside.

The Hambys have added another removable panel to the Secret Panel Chamber.

Lagniappe: While the Tupper Inn no longer operates as a guest house, Jana and Bix Hamby continue to make it their home. Having changed its status from inn back to private residence, they renamed it the John Pope House to honor the original family. The Hambys are exceptional caretakers, ensuring that the house and all its architectural features will be preserved, including one that has created quite a stir. A doorstop for the parlor door is painted the same deep barn-red color of the baseboards, but it does not blend in: it is carved as an anatomically correct representation of the most noticeable part of male genitalia. Hamby has given the antique feature a lot of thought. "I think the Puritan mind, they wouldn't dare do that. I think they gave an assignment to a teenage boy and subconsciously he carved that. These doorstops could have been all over the house, and you could imagine that subsequent generations would have said, 'We can't have that,' and they took them out." Hamby believes that this one survived because it would have been hidden when the parlor door remained open. She speculates that "maybe they left this one because it was just too good." Not everyone is as tolerant as Hamby. "We had a Christmas tour of the house. I was showing this to group after group—four hundred people—but one lady, she jumped back like it was the most horrible thing she had ever seen, and that I had just sinned by bringing it up and disrupting this historic tour." Fortunately, Jana Hamby has a wonderful sense of humor and did not take offense. A renowned children's author and illustrator, she devotes her time and talent to writing and painting in her historic home, leaving the ghosts to come and go as they please.

The Sandwich Glass Museum is home to phantoms William and Rebecca.

5

Phantom Couple on Call

Hannah Rebecca Crowell and William Howes Burgess await the pleasure of your company at the Sandwich Glass Museum. Seek them out, and this phantom couple will share their sad saga.

A faint blush brushed her high cheekbones the first time fifteen-year-old Rebecca (as she preferred to be called) met William Burgess. The dashing, dark-haired sailor stood in the parlor of the home of her wealthy great-uncle Benjamin Burgess. Rebecca, a quiet country girl, had traveled with her parents, Paul and Lydia Crowell, from their West Sandwich home to Boston. Rebecca lowered her thick lashes and tried not to stare when she was introduced to her twenty-year-old distant cousin William, a native of Brewster and already a successful mariner.

William felt equally drawn to the attractive young woman with her shy demeanor. A four-year courtship began as William's sea voyages took him around the globe. Fueled by letters expressing devotion and promises, the couple's mutual admiration grew. In his letters, William wrote of his lofty ideals, his habit of daily prayer, and promised he would never swear in her presence. Rebecca was suitably impressed. Returning from his last port of call, William proposed marriage, and Rebecca accepted. She prepared her hope chest. On August 5, 1852, eighteen-year-old Hannah Rebecca Crowell married twenty-three-year-old William Howes Burgess at the West Sandwich Methodist church. Their rings were engraved with the words "I will never marry again." Dorothy Hogan-Schofield, the curator of the Sandwich Glass Museum, observed that "many people think that Rebecca did this, but it was in fact William." Both William

Hannah Rebecca Crowell Burgess as a young bride.

and Rebecca fulfilled the promise etched in their golden wedding bands—just not the way either had intended.

The couple's ghostly forms appear (as holograms) in the recreated dining room of the Sandwich Glass Museum. The widow Burgess materializes and whispers in a weary voice, "My beloved husband William, God rest his soul. I have missed him for thirty-four years. He was twenty-seven and a captain when he died. I was only his wife for four short years."

Fortunately, Rebecca kept a journal, so the record of what unfolded in the time leading up to William's death has been preserved. Three months after their honeymoon, newlywed William left for sea as the captain of the *Whirlwind*. After a miserable solo journey without his bride, William decided that Rebecca would be with him on all future voyages. On February 4, 1854, the clipper ship *Whirlwind* set sail from New York to San Francisco with husband William at the helm, and wife Rebecca working on her sea

Rebecca, wistful and sad, at her dining room table.

legs. "O how the waves did come over the side of the ship . . . the ship was pitching and rolling and I was not able to walk for fear of falling down. Then I was seasick too . . . it was two weeks before I could even sit up at all. I could scarcely keep my equilibrium."

One night, after she recuperated from her ordeal, William called Rebecca up on deck, and she became enamored with the sea: "I never witnessed such a beautiful sight in my life as tonight at sunset . . . all the colors of the rainbow arranged in fantastic order."

Rebecca was eager to absorb it all, and William took great pleasure in teaching her. "During our first voyage, it took 131 days to travel from Boston to San Francisco . . . yet Rebecca took delight in every aspect of that voyage. Not every woman would set sail with their husband."

For her part, Rebecca had only one issue with the husband she idolized: "I am so happy in love with my husband, yet one thing grieves me; he does not carry out those principles he once professed to sustain." The habit this unreformed sea captain could never overcome? William swore.

Within the first two years of her marriage, Rebecca crossed the equator eleven times and learned to navigate a ship. The experience and acquired skills saved her life and that of thirty crew members on an 1856 voyage around the world on the clipper ship *Challenger,* when William became sick and there was no one to direct the ship.

William had dysentery. With the help of the first mate, Henry Windsor, Rebecca supervised the loading of guano at the Chincha Islands. The crew of the *Challenger* grew increasingly alarmed over the weakened condition of their captain, and Windsor refused to accept responsibility for the ship. Although Rebecca had never captained a vessel, she ordered the anchors up and set sail for Valparaiso, Chile, their next intended port.

For twenty days, Rebecca commanded the ship, taking time only to go below deck to comfort her husband. Tragically, Rebecca was able to hold on to husband's body but not his soul. The specter of William's widow fidgets in the dining room chair. She hesitates before disclosing her beloved's final moments. "We were so happy together, and then my dear husband became gravely ill off the coast of Chile. I loved him so dearly and worked so hard to nurse him back to health."

William died in her arms on December 11, 1856. They were in the Pacific Ocean off the coast of South America. Burial at sea was the customary way to dispose of a body, as it was considered bad luck to have a corpse on board. Rebecca could not bear the thought of tossing William into the fathomless sea, so she held her ground against the superstitious crew and sailed the *Challenger* into Valparaiso with William's body on board.

Rebecca Burgess booked passage on the *Harriet Irving* for herself and her husband's remains. Capt. William Howes Burgess was interred in the Sagamore Cemetery in Sandwich. For the obelisk that serves as his headstone, Rebecca composed a poem. The last verse reads:

Oh! I have loved too fondly
And a gracious Father's hand
Hath removed my cherished idol
To a brighter better land.
But this last hope is left me
To cheer my stricken heart,
In that blest world to meet thee
And never, never part.
Rebecca

More than fifty men offered proposals of marriage to the attractive widow. She spurned them all. William's wedding band, with its engraved vow, remained on her finger until her death at age eighty-two.

William and Rebecca's ghostly images do not appear simultaneously at the Sandwich Glass Museum. Instead, as if in some disconnected dance, they take turns sitting at the head of the table. Unlike his wife, Capt. William Burgess has not aged. His figure takes shape as a robust young man in his late twenties. Dead since 1856, his thoughts rest with his spouse. "My dear wife, Rebecca, she held to our solemn vow never to marry again. Who would have thought I would get so

William, longing to be reunited with Rebecca.

horribly sick at only twenty-seven? There we were, just married, and I the captain of the *Challenger*. We saw places together that most people would only dream about . . . I was so proud of my ship and so in love with Rebecca. We had great plans, she and I."

The transparent apparition in a dark blue captain's jacket is amazed by his wife's grit and courage. "Did you know that as I lay in my sick bed, she managed to navigate the ship back to port. . . . Yes, Rebecca, a woman, what a lady! I knew she was special when I first met her."

As the captain's image starts to fade, his voice catches. His parting words are for Rebecca. "How I wish a place at that table was set for me. How I wish I could come back, take her in my arms, and never let her go. I loved her so very much. May we meet in heaven!"

After burying William, twenty-two-year-old Rebecca continued writing in her journal about her exploits during their brief marriage. Author Megan Taylor Shockley, who wrote about Rebecca, explains that "a lot of Victorian women . . . used their journals to make sense of their lives. What's really important about Rebecca Burgess is that she was able to create an image of herself that people liked, embraced, and wanted to discuss after her death."

Although she "retired from active life," Rebecca enjoyed having close friends and family for dinner and "engaging my guests in conversation."

When making a visit to a reputed haunted site, it is often disappointing when the cadre of ghosts within refuses to make their presence known. At the Sandwich Glass Museum, Rebecca and William are immortalized as holograms, creations of the digital age—a phantom couple eager to make your acquaintance.

Lagniappe: Finding Rebecca and William can be a bit tricky. Navigating the warren of fifteen exhibit rooms in the Sandwich

An amazing array of colors and shapes in the museum.

Museum requires perseverance. More than six thousand glass objects in brilliant hues of ruby red, royal amethyst, canary yellow, cobalt blue, pearl pink, opalescent white, and emerald green are mesmerizing. Distractions are at every turn, each goblet a regal chalice to observe, each Lacy plate, a coronet for the gods. Some visitors go full circle, exit through the gift shop, and never meet the delightful couple. To avoid the same mistake, use the guided map, and steer the circuitous route. Bypass the glassblowing demonstration, the Introduction to the Story of Glass, the Mixing Room, and the Hirschmann Theatre. Enter and exit the *Art of the Glass Blower* exhibit, and then make a sharp right from the Mold-Blown and Early Press Glass Rooms into the Lacy Glass area. From there, look to the left for the entrance to Mid-Nineteenth Century Pressed Glass. Keep going straight through Pattern Glass, and make a hard right. Look overhead for the sign that reads "The Hannah Rebecca Burgess Dining Room." If you find yourself in Post-Civil War Production or Threaded and Decorated Glass, you have gone too far. The entrance will be dark, but feel for the top blue button, and press it. Have a seat on the bench, be patient, and in a few moments, you will hear a woman gasp: "Oh, you are not my dinner guests!" Ever the gracious hostess, Rebecca's hologram comes into focus as she announces, "Let me light the lamps and candles so we can see each other." And so her story begins.

6

Gaffers, Ghosts, and the Glassmakers' Ball

Long ago, the blowing-iron designated the glassmaker King of Fire and Air. . . . the Spirit of Glass has lived on through the ages, appearing in multifold guises.
—Frank W. Chipman, *The Romance of Old Sandwich Glass*

The site of the Boston and Sandwich Glass Factory in the village of Jarvesville harbors a few tall tales, a bewitching spell where glass creations came to life, and a glassblower with a paranormal talent for appearing and disappearing at will. The tales grasp at the tenuous hold of fact over fiction.

Founded in 1825 by Deming Jarves, the Boston and Sandwich Glass Factory transformed the remote fishing and farming community of Sandwich. By the 1850s, five hundred workers produced more than five million pieces of glass annually, and the Sandwich factory was one of the largest producers of glassware in the country. The "gaffers," as master glassblowers were then known, were considered the foremost craftsmen of the nineteenth century. They belonged to a "superstitiously secretive trade" with origins tracing back some five thousand years.

The Egyptians had glassblowers, as did the Greeks and Romans. In Venice, doges conferred noble titles on these magicians who conjured up breathtaking shapes by breathing life into glass tubes. For his factory to succeed, to surpass the output of other glass houses, Deming Jarves needed skilled artisans. He brought in the best gaffers from England, Ireland, and France, and they in turn brought the "spirit of glass" with them.

A glowing goblet that lures its beholder.

The "magic potions" of the glass gaffer.

Directed by the gaffers, an ensemble of workers scurried to their assigned tasks. Sitting on overturned nail kegs, two stoop-shouldered chipmasters meticulously chipped off flakes of thin glass that adhered to the openings of bottles, lamps, and decanters. Young boys, the rosin monkeys, tossed scoops of pulverized rosin into the hungry furnace to keep the fires lit as the mold boys juggled iron tongs to seize the molds from the fire.

As children of the Cape, these youngsters had grown up with many legendary tales, stories of mythical sea creatures that sank ships and of Squant, the sea woman with green hair and a body sleek and flat like ribbons of kelp. So powerful was Squant's magic that she lured the Wampanoag giant Maushop into her underwater cave, never to escape. Of course they were familiar with glass witch balls, which, when hung in a window, could ward off disasters.

Yet, the strange stories of the aging chipmasters brought the realm of the unknown into the drudgery of their day-to-day existence. The

Recreations of a chipmaster and a gaffer in the factory.

The recreation of a young mold boy tending the fire.

young apprentices crept as close as they dared to learn more about one of their own—a gaffer who could cast spells and make a glass bell ring by itself on the hour or create a dazzling glass flower that opened when the sun shone on it and gave forth a sweet perfume. Most bizarre of all was this gaffer's ability to fashion a singular cloudy, ruby-red glass flower that, when held in a virgin's hand, turned crystal clear. The impressionable boys turned to gaffer Bonique, the cleverest glassblower in the factory, who could shape the molten glass into wondrous forms. Bonique staunchly maintained that he was not the creator of these miraculous glass pieces.

Of all the odd men with off-Cape ways at the factory, Adolphe Bonique stood out as the most peculiar. The chipmasters whispered that he might be the son of a French nobleman who had escaped the deadly guillotines of the French Revolution. When the pair of gossiping old men began to weave another tale, that Bonique had served as Napoleon's military strategist, gaffers Nicholas Lutz from

A glass flower that gives off a mysterious perfume.

Glass "whimsies" created by the gaffers.

Germany and Englishman Robert Matthews intervened; they told the chipmasters that fumes from the furnace had addled their brains.

Still, the rosin and mold boys believed that Bonique was no ordinary man. He might wear the same homespun breeches as the rest of the workmen, but there were rumors that Bonique was rich, a descendant of one of the sixty Acadian exiles whose boats sailed into Buzzards Bay. Taken as prisoners and made into indentured servants by a few unscrupulous Cape Codders, the Acadians managed to conceal a horde of gold before they were captured—and Bonique knew where to find it. Why then, the young boys asked each other, did Bonique work among them? If he had the gold of kings, why slave in the heat of their humble factory?

Factory owner Deming Jarves paid no heed to rumors. His passion was glass. An astute businessman, Jarves believed that happy workers were productive workers. He provided affordable housing clustered near the factory in Jarvesville. There was a four-day work week. During off hours, workers were allowed to create and keep glass "whimsies," novelty items such as bells, bellows, banks, bears, rolling pins, pipes, top hats, toys, and glass walking canes, for their own amusement or as gifts. Jarves gave out treats to the children on the Fourth of July and Christmas. The adults looked forward to the annual Glassmakers Masquerade Ball.

During those prosperous years when Cape Cod sea captains were bringing back the riches of the seven seas and orders for Sandwich Glass were pouring in, the workers were eager to celebrate. Residents of Jarvesville created costumes for the ball, and delicate glass flowers were hand-stitched on gowns. The chipmasters tamed their wild gray beards and donned new breeches and coats. They all were disappointed that Bonique would not be there to see them at their best. The surprisingly female-shy master gaffer had fled to the dwindling woods around Sandwich.

On the evening of the ball, the chipmasters, both amazingly agile dancers, basked in the attention showered on them by the females in attendance. Just as they were bragging that they knew of a strange, secret process, where the blue of the Nauset Sea could be caught and held forever in the stem of a goblet of wine, a masked stranger commanded the center of the dance floor. Elegantly attired in a white brocade coat with a dazzling glass ruby star pinned to a blue ribbon across his chest, the handsome gentleman glanced about the ballroom, bowed to the ladies, and took his leave. His mysterious departure was as abrupt as his arrival.

In the predawn hours, the two chipmasters staggered home. Residents of Jarvesville slipped their sore feet beneath the covers. If any among them had awakened to shutter a window, they might have seen a regal figure strolling down the deserted street. He had a curious habit of pausing before a few doors, and then rapping gently on them with a golden glass cane.

In the morning, as the weary workers straggled into the factory, Bonique already had his iron in the fire of the glory hold, slowly rotating the molten glass. The chipmasters rested their aching bones on the nail kegs, but their wagging tongues were not stilled. The stranger who had "materialized" in the center of the dance floor must have been Bonique, who could "shift-shape" from mortal man to immortal specter. The phantom Bonique came to relive his royal lifestyle but "disappeared" just as quickly, once he realized that the Sandwich Glassmakers Ball was but a poor caricature of the magnificent galas he had once attended at palatial palaces.

In *Romance of Old Sandwich Glass,* Frank W. Chipman, whose father and grandfather both worked at the glass factory, instills a sense that Sandwich glass possessed a certain magic—"it lures the fancy of the beholder," and its creators were powerful conjurers. "It seems that a halo of the unusual always has been attached to the occupation of the glassmaker."

Folklorist Elizabeth Reynard maintained that on the anniversary of the Glassmakers Ball, the soft lilting echo of fiddles floats over the night air, and, at dawn, a phantom parade led by a "slender figure . . . transparent as glass," strolls the streets near the old factory. The ghost is tall, gallant, and debonair. "Any girl would take him for a lover in a dream."

Those blessed with a sixth sense may still witness the alluring spirit

Sandwich glass with its charmed properties.

as he strides through the fog of a Cape Cod evening and knocks on village doors with his golden glass cane. Walking behind the phantom gaffer Bonique are the swaggering ghosts of two old men. According to Reynard, "One would think that the figure before them . . . was a puppet of their creating, like the crystal bells that ring the hour, and the glass flowers that open in the sun."

Lagniappe: Sandwich Glass, with its charmed properties and luminous colors, is no longer made. The warning *caveat emptor* holds particularly true for those seeking to own a piece of this artistic history, as reproductions flood the market. Displays at the Sandwich Glass Museum, owned and operated by the Sandwich Historical Society, on Main Street allow visitors to appreciate and marvel at the artistry of the glassblower. "The Factory was operated not merely for financial gain, but . . . to create glass with a soul," states Chipman. The Boston and Sandwich Glass Factory ceased

The site of the former Sandwich glass factory.

The "map" that plots the footsteps of the gaffers, chipmasters, rosin monkeys, and mold boys.

operation on New Year's Day 1888. There were a few futile attempts to revive production under new ownership, but, in 1907, the fire in the furnace was extinguished, never to be relit. The factory buildings were slowly dismantled in the 1920s and 1940s.

In a clearing at the corner of Factory and Jarves Streets in Jarvesville, a simple concrete block with a bronze plaque commemorates the site of the "glass factory that built a town." Aged to a pale verdigris patina, the raised design of the plaque contains a compelling diagram—a map to be treasured. Here curious fingers can retrace the footsteps of the gaffers, chipmasters, rosin monkeys, and mold boys through the labyrinth of the old factory. In the quiet of the clearing, listen for the chatter of two old men spinning their never-ending tales.

The Isaiah Thomas Rare Bookstore in Cotuit.

7

The Extraordinary Bookstore

A rare-book store evokes a certain aura of decorum, a refined dignity in accord with the priceless tomes gracing its shelves—but the Isaiah Thomas Rare Book Store in Cotuit is not that place. Outside, the rambling Victorian house nearly stops traffic with its shocking pink façade.

Inside, a bust of Shakespeare sprouts Mickey Mouse ears, and its shoulders sport a short, white, fur cape. In the children's section, a large, one-eyed teddy bear, dressed in pink velour Lederhosen, perches on a sofa, and a golden, six-foot papier-mâché King Tut

A one-eyed teddy bear, wearing Lederhosen, in the children's section.

Shakespeare's bust dons Mickey Mouse ears.

A papier mâché King Tut sarcophagus guards the stacks.

sarcophagus stands upright between the stacks. Amid the tchotchkes, first editions, art prints, and amazing collection of seventy thousand books, there has been enough poltergeist activity to tantalize any avid ghost hunter.

Bookstore owner Jim Visbeck has been around for most of it. "One of the most unusual things really is this clock." He gestures to a battery-operated pendulum clock mounted on the wall that separates the front room from the next. There is nothing particularly remarkable about the golden-oak case with its oval glass door, brass face with black hour and minute hands, or circular brass pendulum. Before continuing his story, Visbeck deflects the clock's paranormal abilities by stating, "There has to be a physical explanation for it. Maybe this is out of balance. I've never had a level on it." He shakes his thick head of graying hair, stares at the offending timepiece, and then picks up the tale. "Many, many years ago, we came home after three weeks on the road in March about nine-thirty at night, and

Jim Visbeck, surrounded by books, tchotchkes, and the mysterious clock.

The haunted clock arbitrarily stops.

we're punching the alarm, and the clock had stopped—at least, the pendulum had stopped at the very time we came in, so it seems."

If this had been the only instance, the book dealer would have brushed it off. "But," says Visbeck, "it's been going on and on." The atypical clock marks certain comings and goings by arbitrarily stopping. "I swear we would go to a book fair in New Hampshire, Vermont, Boston, it didn't matter. We'd come back home late at night and the clock would stop when we came in."

The bookstore occupies the ground floor, and Visbeck and his partner reside upstairs. He shrugs off the notion that the clock objects to being left alone. "My buddy was upstairs, he came down to say something to my assistant and me, and the clock just stopped. Last summer, there was a conference on ghosty things up at the Cape Cod Community College, and two people came here, independent of each other, but obviously for the same purpose: to find out if my clock was haunted somehow. One left, and then the other started up the same conversation. I was telling her about this clock, and it stopped."

Visbeck even tried putting the clock to a test. "I am coming over the bridge four or five years ago, and I said out loud, 'I wonder if the clock will stop when I get back?' It didn't." The puzzled book store owner can't figure out what triggers its bizarre behavior. "I don't know, maybe if you step on the floorboards near it, it jars the clock?" Visbeck doesn't accept that theory either, as the clock has stopped when they open the front door, a room away. "Of course, ever since I sort of acknowledged it, it hasn't done it again."

Like many older buildings on the Cape, this nineteenth-century house, originally built as a private residence for Zenas Crocker in 1861, has a patchy history. "We bought it in 1989. Before that, it was a woman's clothing store called the Sail Loft. There was a sun porch they used as dressing rooms. Upstairs was sort of offices and storage, and this was basically all open, except there was a salon area here. It was a real estate office and the Nickerson Funeral Home."

Visbeck waves his arm towards an L-shaped counter topped with stacks of books and knickknacks. "My desk is where the body would be viewed, and there is a fireplace over there that I just covered up."

Visbeck's desk area, where caskets and bodies were viewed during the building's time as a funeral home.

He indicates a room to the left. A three-foot-tall dragon gargoyle with mouth agape guards the entrance. "This was a sitting room, and I am sure they put in those two big double doors, which are entirely out of character in the other room, so they could bring a body in." He enumerates further evidence from its days as a funeral parlor. "In the back was a shed that was tacked on with a different sort of cellar; it came with a rubber floor and a drain." The antiquarian book dealer rattles off the details, and then continues the tour with scattered references to a pesky poltergeist.

"At some point, the house was divided into sections and rented out." He stops near the front wall facing the street. "Behind this closet and to the left were the fireplace and the maid's stairs. Those doors were open, and there were a couple of apartments upstairs."

When word got out that the rare-book shop might be harboring ghosts, the former renters returned to share their stories. "People

The former entrance to the sitting room of the Nickerson Funeral Parlor.

would come back and tell me these crazy things. One said, 'My girl-friend and I were in nursing school, and we rented this place for a month in the summertime. She told us about funny things happening.' Her roommate got pushed down the maid's stairs when she was sweeping them. The roommate insisted, 'I wasn't clumsy. I was pushed.'"

As Visbeck worked on renovations to the second floor, converting it back to a private residence, he noticed a few more peculiarities, including the refinished spaces upstairs. "When we first got here, my bedroom is over there, and Hank's bedroom is over here, and the front room is there, and for ten years we had a little galley kitchen. We sat on the floor or on the sofa, and our table was the coffee table. I had better knees then." The owner laughs at his limitations. "So, one morning, I am putting water on for tea, and I just walked past the sofa." Visbeck snaps his head sharply to the side, repeating the reaction he had that day. "And this lady was sitting there, high collar on her dress, gray hair. I did a double take, and told myself to go wash your face, take a shower, dismiss it." When he looked back, the female spirit was gone.

A neighbor and an old picture offered clues to the identity of the early morning visitor. "Merle Crocker, a descendant of the original owners, had passed in 2003, and his widow, Jean Crocker, had just gone into assisted living. I went to her estate sale and bought this picture." The black-and-white photograph from 1874 shows Zenas Crocker III and his family posing in front of the house, which he built with Gold Rush money. Gathered on the front lawn with Zenas are his wife, Susan, and their sons, Zenas Crocker IV and Francis. The daughters stand slightly distant, Helen behind her parents, and Hattie by the fence close to the road. Inside the house, one anomaly hinted at a disturbed soul, giving any of these females—Susan, Helen, or Hattie—motivation to return in spirit form.

"There is a little room at the peak that you can only get up to from the other side of that fireplace, where an even smaller set of stairs goes almost straight up, and you have to crawl because if you put your head up, you would knock it, kill yourself because of the nails sticking out. At the top of the stairs, there is an unfinished room. You could stand up over there, and this is what the door looked like." Visbeck sketches an oddly-outfitted door. "And there were latches on the outside and a peep hole. When we opened the door, the room was covered in mattresses." The mattress-covered room was disturbing, especially when Visbeck remembered what Jean Crocker had told him when he purchased the old photo of the house. "She said that one of the inhabitants early on was mentally ill, and this is the 1860s to 1880s. You don't know how people treated slow people at that time."

In trying to make a connection between the house, the mattress-covered room, and the female ghost who appeared in his living quarters, Visbeck sorts through what he knows. "It was a young lady who was ill who lived here. I was just thinking it could be her, somebody who was a little upset with things, not sure what is going on anymore. But the woman I saw on the second floor didn't seem like a young person."

The mattress-lined room was discovered under this peak.

The even-tempered book dealer would like to dismiss the entire paranormal/poltergeist concept as "all crap," but too much has happened. "When I first moved in here, I had never heard anything about spirits being here. There are probably ordinary reasons why all this is going on. I try to ignore things now." Yet, turning a blind eye has proved impossible, as the ghost of Zenas Crocker's former house is fond of late night visits.

"Half the time, I swear, I don't even open my eyes anymore when I feel a depression at the foot of the bed. I do have cats, and one of the cats, Callie, usually sleeps with me." Anticipating the logical next question, Visbeck quickly inserts, "Of course, the cats do bounce and walk across the bed, but there is a distinct difference between the depression and cats. All of a sudden, it just goes down, as if someone is sitting and joining me at the foot of the bed. Sometimes I have the cat right next to me, and I can feel the depression but the cat doesn't."

Another strange instance of the poltergeist phenomenon could also be blamed on the cats, but the trajectory of the flying objects doesn't support a kitty stampede. "I have a number of collections," says Visbeck, stating the obvious, "so we put in knee-high bookcases where the ceiling slants down at an angle upstairs," finally giving the avid collector a place to display his favorites. "I am carrying and carrying boxes; it took a couple of weeks to get it all up here, unpacked, and arranged the way I want. It's two-thirty in the morning, and I'm finally done." Visbeck recalls elatedly wiping his hand across his brow once, twice. "Then, something goes crash in the kitchen. Now the kitchen cabinets . . . have open space above them. I have a glass bud vase up there that has glass flowers—white ones with candles—and it crashes down, but doesn't break." Visbeck considers that either of the cats could have done it, as there is a spiral staircase that leads up to that level in order to access a "little half-door into the attic." The cats could have "crossed over on a beam that supports the dormer," but even though cats are agile, he thinks it would be a stretch. When Visbeck ran into the kitchen, there were no cats in sight. Hoping to dissuade the "ghost" from similar future actions, he made a little announcement: "All right, you can stay here, but don't break anything. Geez!"

The ghost took Visbeck up on his offer of permanent residency, but performed one final feat of prestidigitation. "I had a wonderful little framed etching, about five by seven, a little girl sort of laying down reading, and that's propped up on a shelf down here. Then, at an antique shop, I found a small, fist-size bronze of a boy reading—they are perfect together. I placed her behind him, and one morning around three o'clock, I heard this crash loud enough that I heard it in my bedroom on the other side of the house. It woke me up." The building has an alarm system, and the store was "all buttoned up. If anybody got in, then the alarm would jangle throughout the place." Still the owner checked downstairs and couldn't find anyone or anything amiss. "Then the next day, I saw my little girl picture lying flat, straight down on the floor with the little bronze figure safely on the shelf." Visbeck remains in disbelief. "Somehow, the etching flew up and over the statue." He'd like to blame it on the cats, who had never previously knocked over his "googas or knickknacks," but he knows the angle is all wrong and their aim could never be that good.

Visbeck hopes that since he "acknowledged that there is *somebody* here, it's all she wants. Just, sort of, show a little respect, and then you don't have any issues." It has worked so far. Nothing has broken recently, and the loud crashes have ceased. The proprietor of the Isaiah Thomas Rare Book Store has even turned down Hollywood. "At first I thought it was a ruse. This production company called me to have ghost hunters come and film an investigation here, and I said, 'No, thanks.' I told them, 'I don't deny it, but I don't want to be known as the haunted book store.' We're a serious book store: I have a signed *Gone with the Wind,* and a signed *Atlas Shrugged,* and the first English *Harry Potter.* " Jim Visbeck prefers to have customers focused on literary material. An obsession for books he can deal with; ghosts, not so much. One of his favorite plaques advises:

Warning! Rare Book Pox Highly Contagious! There is no known cure! Infection is characterized by dizziness, sweaty palms and compulsive reading of rare books . . . accompanied by apnea and lust. Further symptoms are: loss of home living space and self-induced poverty. If infected do not see your doctor, but seek aid from your local antiquarian book dealer, who, while unable to affect a cure, can provide symptomatic relief.

Lagniappe: Located on Falmouth Road (Route 28), the Isaiah Thomas Rare Book Store is named in honor of revolutionary-era printer and philanthropist, Isaiah Thomas, the founder of the American Antiquarian Society (AAS) in 1812. Jim Visbeck is a member of the Antiquarian Booksellers Association of America (ABAA), the International League of Antiquarian Booksellers (ILAB), and the Massachusetts and Rhode Island Antiquarian Booksellers (MARIAB), so painting his establishment a shocking pink seems out of character. The proprietor agrees—sort of. "My original partner's wife was a long-time art teacher, a graduate of Massachusetts College of Art. We decided to do several kinds of things at once: we added one thousand feet on three different levels—it made my living space wonderful. I can put fifty people up there, and I have for parties for book sellers. So when it came time to do all of this, we faced the front so the wood was all new and natural and had to be painted. There are wonderful books on Victorian houses, and she chose the colors. At the time, I didn't know if I would want to live in a pink house, but then she said, 'Well, let's try.'" Visbeck wouldn't have it any other way now, but there were repercussions. He measures out his next words slowly. "No one ever came to me personally to object, but a couple of times I was in line at the supermarket, and people would grumble: 'What are they doing? Pepto-Bismol pink and all that.' Then, the owner of the Regatta Restaurant across the street, which is another historic Crocker house, said, 'Leave it alone. It looks good.' Well, you know," says a philosophical Visbeck, "any notice is good notice. Maybe I've started a trend."

The Crocker Tavern House on Old King's Highway.

8

A Woman's Work Is Never Done

Oh, the shrewdness of their shrewdness when they're shrewd,
And the rudeness of their rudeness when they're rude;
But the shrewdness of their shrewdness and the rudeness of their rudeness,
Are as nothing to their goodness when they're good.

—Anonymous

Although the majority of the Crocker Tavern's patrons were male, Lydia's ghost grabs the spotlight. In 1774, patriots gathered at the Crocker Tavern in Barnstable to plot their freedom. As a "public" house along Old King's Highway, tavern keeper Cornelius Crocker also had to contend with the equally passionate opposition of the Tories, those loyal to England. Politics and booze are a volatile mix—angry fists hammered the wooden tables, and ale sloshed out of pewter tankards as heated debate carried through the nights. Little Lydia Crocker watched from the sidelines.

Following the death of her father, Cornelius, in 1784, Lydia Crocker Sturgis inherited the tavern. Lydia Crocker had married Samuel Sturgis on April 3, 1760. Two years later, at age twenty-three, she became a widow. The widow Sturgis rose to become a prominent force in the village, and town meetings were held at "Aunt Lydia's Tavern." Lydia's ghost is often regarded as "the caretaker." Nothing escapes her scrutiny.

Anne Carlson, who operates the eighteenth-century historic structure as a vacation rental home with her husband is happy that she has had only one run-in with Lydia. "Thirteen years ago, we bought the house from a couple who coincidentally also had the last name of Carlson. They were running it as a bed and breakfast.

We asked them if the house was haunted and they said no." Anne hesitates. "Quickly, we learned that Aunt Lydia is the main ghost, and she acts like a caretaker. She's the one everyone talks about. They even featured her in a Halloween special on Home and Garden TV."

Carlson is in full Halloween mode, scooping up pumpkins in the store for her home off the Cape. It brings back memories of hectic days prepping the Crocker Tavern House for its opening as a vacation rental home.

"I had ordered a bunch of mattresses, and I had the doors open because we had men all over the house in the bedrooms, upstairs and down, moving in mattresses. I had my caretaker with me who had been with us at another property to check out some of the things we needed done. All of a sudden, the back door slammed shut, and there was no wind, no one was near the back door—everyone was inside in the bedrooms installing mattresses. We couldn't figure out why this was happening." Carlson and her caretaker went to check the back door. "It actually locked, and even though we tried to recreate it, slamming it and slamming it, we could never get this hook and eye to go into this slot to actually lock the same way it had happened the first time. It didn't seem possible, but the lock locked itself." A resigned Carlson gave up. "We did attribute it to Aunt Lydia. I stood there and said, 'Okay, I don't believe in you, but if you are actually here, if you approve of everything that I am doing in running this property, then I don't want to see you again!'" Carlson feels she must be doing something right because "I've never had to deal with Aunt Lydia again. I guess she just didn't like all the doors being left open."

Derek Bartlett leads a popular evening ghost tour through Barnstable Village. Anxious whispers and nervous giggles float in the air. When Bartlett stops, his tour goers knock into each other like bumper cars with underage drivers. The tour guide waits patiently by the red front door of the Crocker Tavern House. "This was the meeting place for the Whig Party during Colonial times, and it's had its share of paranormal activities."

A dozen flashlights shine on the door, windows, and even the shrubs in a battle to be the first to spot a ghost. Bartlett settles the group down with a warning. "Ghosts, like people, don't like to be chased." The flashlights click off. "This was a museum for a while, until a couple from Pennsylvania turned it into a B&B. The husband is alone while his wife is out shopping for groceries. He hears a woman outside screaming 'Help me! Help me!' He runs out the front door and looks up and down Kings Highway for a woman who might be injured. He sees no one, finds no one. His wife pulls up with the groceries. He runs over and tells her about the woman screaming for help, but he can't find her. The wife puts her bag of groceries on the hood of the car, smiles at him and says, 'Honey, I've been hearing this woman scream all week. She's not outside, she's inside the house.'"

Now that he has their attention, Bartlett presses on. "A woman is staying in Aunt Lydia's room. She wakes up and standing over her bed is an elderly woman in a dress and bonnet. The guest screams, closes her eyes, reopens her eyes, and the ghost has disappeared." He recommends this technique: "If you are frightened by a ghost, close your eyes and scream really loud. When you open your eyes again the ghost will be gone."

Before moving on, Bartlett tells one final story. "One night while I was giving this tour, we stopped here, and the family renting the house invited us to come in, and they had a ghost story to tell us. They were in the west wing, and the night before, the wife was sitting on the bed, and the husband was across the room taking his watch off and putting it on the dresser. From the empty space between them, they heard a voice crying 'Help me! Help me!'" A teenager in the group asks if it's Aunt Lydia, and the guide responds that ghosts unfortunately are not in the habit of identifying themselves.

Current owner Anne Carlson shakes her head. "I've heard the story of the woman crying 'Help me! Help me!,' but neither my husband nor I have heard her or any other voices in the house that shouldn't be here."

For Carlson, far more exciting events, based on historical facts, have transpired at the former tavern. "It happened in our barn.

A British soldier walked in and didn't realize that the Whigs [the patriots] met on our property. There was a sword fight, and he jabbed and missed. His sword got stuck in a beam, and so one of the Whigs was able to stab him. Different people have claimed to have had experiences with his ghost." The heated barn is now used for parties, banquets, and conferences. The notch that was cut during the sword fight is visible on an overhead beam.

The Carlsons have named the various bedrooms after historical figures associated with the house or with the founding of the nation: Cornelius Crocker, Aunt Lydia Crocker, James Otis, Mercy Otis Warren, George Washington, John Adams, and James Madison. Barnstable's patriotic campaign culminated when the Cape Cod militia gathered in front of the Crocker Tavern to march to Lexington and Concord to fight for American independence. The spirit of one of these brave men seems to be fighting to return. A guest staying in the James Otis room swore that he saw the outline of a soldier walk across his room and then vanish in the shadows.

An encounter between British and Patriot soldiers took place in the barn.

A vacation rental just minutes from the beach, the spacious, seven-bedroom home is ideally suited for large groups and family reunions, but one couple staying in Aunt Lydia's room had to make room for one more.

During the night, the wife rolled over to cuddle with her husband but found herself bumped up against a stranger. Reaching her hand back to the left side of the bed, she realized she was wedged between two men. She calmed down enough to tug at her husband's shoulder. He propped himself up, leaned over his wife, and saw nothing. The uninvited "bedmate" was gone. Since the ghost did not return on the second night, the couple assumed that the ghost realized he wasn't welcome. "I guess he was as shocked as I was to find the bed already occupied."

Reputedly, Aunt Lydia's room has the most supernatural activity. A soothing night's rest is often interrupted by the violent shaking of the bed. If it is former proprietor Lydia, she's doing some heavy-duty lifting as the room features a massive antique double-bed with canopy.

Lydia Crocker Sturgis passed the business on to her daughter Sally. Sally married Daniel Crocker. When Daniel died in 1811, his widow stepped in and the "Sally Crocker Tavern" served libations until 1837. After decades as a popular alehouse, the building became a private residence. In 1927, the Crocker family sold the property to the Society for the Preservation of New England Antiquities. The Society operated it as a museum, showcasing "the affluent sector of colonial life on olde Cape Cod" until the 1960s. The Society imposed restrictions on future owners to protect the Georgian and Federal style architectural features. However, buyers did not rush forward, and the tavern, once a magnet for passionate oratory in favor of American liberty, sat idle. It is from this period that the haunted tales began.

In the second decade of the twenty-first century, the raucous shouts of tavern patrons have dissipated, and vacationers staying at the Crocker Tavern House are eager to learn about its place in American history. One guest wrote an almost glowing review. "The

Barnstable's haunted Old Gaol.

home is utterly charming, a reminder of our rich heritage—except for the ghosts."

Lagniappe: Crocker Tavern House in Barnstable is in the Old King's Highway Historic District, along with the Old Colonial Courthouse, the Sturgis Library, the Village Schoolhouse, and the Old Gaol (jail). Built in 1690, the jail is said to be the oldest wooden prison structure in the United States, and it has its ghosts. It served as the town jail until around 1820 when a new stone jail was built. The old jail was repurposed as a barn, and in 1972, it was moved to its present location next to the Coast Guard Heritage Museum. The jail is the final stop on the Derek Bartlett's ghost hunting tour. A shadowy figure has been seen moving around the first floor of the jail and standing by the ladder that leads to the second story loft, where confinement cells were located. The cells still have their original iron bars, hinges, locks, and graffiti. In his book about the prison, author

The jail cells in the loft where prisoners were kept.

John Paul De Milio remembers touring the jail and seeing a carving of a sailing vessel on the cell wall. He speculates that it must have been a source of comfort, a symbol of freedom, for the person who created it. A few other locals have suggested that the carving was made by one of the pirates who survived the 1717 shipwrecks of the *Whydah* and the *Marianne* off of Cape Cod. The pirates were confined in the old Barnstable jail for their trial and subsequent hangings in Boston. Also locked in the jail were those deemed mad or insane. At the conclusion of the ghost tour, an invitation is extended to those brave enough to stand inside the cell area in the dark. Bartlett informs the group that digital recorders have captured the voices of former prisoners "Joel" and "Mary." Whether ghostly voices are heard or not, the oppressive atmosphere of the old jail gives off a dark sense of foreboding—and a strong desire for fresh air and freedom.

9

The Ghost House

Behind every man now alive stands thirty ghosts, for that is the ratio by which the dead outnumber the living.

—Sir Arthur C. Clarke,
from the foreword to *2001: A Space Odyssey*

Eleven lively spirits are said to lurk in and about the Barnstable House. From the outside, the early eighteenth-century house appears to be a typical two-story colonial. The interior, used for office space, is just as innocuous. Yet, it is a favorite haunt of spirits young and old.

The Barnstable House, home to eleven ghosts.

Six-year-old Lucy is a playful spirit. She bounces her ball down the stairs and dances around the conference room table (formerly the dining room). Little Lucy drowned in her own home in the river that ran under the house.

Early records indicate that the house was constructed in Scituate, Massachusetts in 1713, and then floated by barge to Barnstable in 1716, which may account for the numbers mounted in black on the chimney stack. James Paine chose to build the foundation over the underground river for easy access to fresh water. A hole was dug in the cellar, and it was a simple matter of lowering a bucket to draw up a sufficient supply for cooking, bathing, and cleaning. James and his wife, Bethiah, could never have foreseen that their darling daughter would fall in and drown.

One version of the tale recounts Lucy bouncing her favorite blue ball in the cellar when it rolled into the hole, and she fell in while trying to retrieve it. A prevailing paranormal theory holds that when a child dies tragically, his or her spirit will return to the place where they were the most comfortable. Visitors have reported sounds of childish giggles coming from the second floor bedroom.

Hoping soon to be reunited with her child, the grieving spirit of Lucy's mother rocks her sorrows away in a chair by the fireplace. Over the years, people have said that they've seen the chair rock by itself and "phantom fires" flare up in the hearth.

When Dr. Samuel Savage purchased the former Paine home in 1772, rumors circulated that this skilled physician dabbled in the occult, that the good doctor had found a way to open the door to the spirit world, enabling spirits to travel back and forth at will. Such knowledge and ability lends certain credence to the stories of the doctor's spirit paying a few house calls in the afterlife. As the Spiritualist movement, with its practice of communicating with the dead, was beginning to make inroads in the United States, Dr. Savage's side practice as a medium might not have seemed that strange.

A commemorative eulogy published in the August 1833 edition of *New England Magazine* praised the doctor as a man of "sterling character and penetrating judgment" with "kind attention and unwearied exertions for his patients [that] were returned by devoted reverence, and unlimited confidence in his superior skills." It was also noted that "he was impatient of contradiction, and . . . little respected sentiments opposite of his own . . . he sternly rebuked hypocrisy and boldly censured the least semblance of deception."

Dr. George N. Munsell of Harwich remembered his fellow physician as a man of eccentricities. "He was very peculiar in his manners, and when the stage coach was passing, he would ascend a large rock, which is still there, and in sepulchral tones announce himself as a physician and surgeon."

Neighborhood children dreaded going near the doctor's house for fear he might be outside "seated in his round-about chair" on the porch. According to Fred Rogers in the *Journal of the History of Medicine and Allied Sciences,* "The girl who ventured to pass without curtsying, or boy without removing his cap, were sure to be brought to bay by a rap on the floor with his cane and a hail that youthful temerity dared not pass unheeded." Twenty-first-century trick-or-treaters would do well to avoid the Barnstable House on Halloween; the disposition of the doctor's ghost would likely be as cranky now as when he was alive.

Accounts of Dr. Savage's stern visage and forceful personality might have played a role in the creation of the tyrannical Captain Ahab in Herman Melville's *Moby Dick.* Melville is said to have written part of this classic novel at Barnstable House. His stepmother-in-law was Hope Savage Shaw, the daughter of Dr. Samuel Savage.

After the Savage family moved out, Capt. John Grey moved in. When the private residence was converted to a commercial establishment in the 1950s, it operated as Captain Grey's Inn. Professional ghost hunter Derek Bartlett says that the ill-tempered captain died here and that he and his loyal servant haunt the property. Both would prefer to be left alone. Dinner guests at Captain Grey's Inn registered an assortment of complaints: unseen hands yanked off the tablecloth in front of them, a water pitcher levitated above the table and then came crashing down, a chair flipped over backwards. The constant jarring thuds of doors slamming over their heads prompted one elderly couple to leave before dessert arrived. They said the food was delicious, but they couldn't "deal with all the antics."

Renovated and under new management, Captain Grey's Inn became the Barnstable House, and less cantankerous spirits emerged. The wait staff reported that as they came out of the kitchen balancing full trays, they would bump into a man in a yellow, double-breasted frock coat and breeches. He would bow from the waist and wave them on. A cute little girl with brown ringlets would dart between the tables then vanish. The owner of the restaurant allowed séances, in which psychics assured him that all of the resident spirits were friendly.

A fire in the 1970s brought out another spirit, who has come to be known as Martha. Smoke billowed from the third story attic windows as the fire trucks arrived. Three of the firemen looked up to see a woman peering out. She had long, blonde hair and what they later described as a white nightgown. They rushed up the stairs but were unable to find her or anything that could have been mistaken for a woman—not even a mannequin—posed in the window. After the fire was extinguished, a fireman was wrapping up the hose when he was approached by a young woman. He thought it odd that she would be out on such a snowy evening without a coat. He was about to suggest she find warmer attire when he glanced at her bare feet and saw that she was levitating above the ground. Martha's story is now part of local lore, with many variations. The most dramatic of these tales involves Martha floating from the flames in the burning window down to the ground.

In the 1980s, the restaurant closed its doors for the last time. The Barnstable House once again underwent a conversion; this time into office space. Bartlett's ghost tour stops here after office hours. The building is dark, and all the businesses are closed. The ghost guide challenges any one in his group to go up and knock on the door and see if there is a corresponding rap from a spirit inside.

Bartlett throws one more ghost into the mix. He points to a telephone pole at the edge of the property. Lurking in the murky shadows is the ghost of Edmund Hawes, who, as a man, lived in the

Martha's ghost is said to float from this window.

A young girl listens at the door for the sounds of ghosts inside.

house after the Paine family but before Dr. Savage. Hawes lost his entire fortune when the value of his colonial currency declined, and he hanged himself from a tree on the property. His despondent ghost never ventures into the house, but prowls restlessly from where the tree had been to the front door.

The ghost tally approaches eleven. Counting ghosts is like keeping track of passing clouds, shape-shifting puffs trailing across an endless sky—they come, they go, drifting from one sphere to the next.

Lagniappe: After the fire in the 1970s and after the Barnstable House ceased operation as a restaurant in the 1980s, little Lucy's ghost sought new companionship. In the center of town, across from the Barnstable County Courthouse, where orator Daniel Webster argued cases, a new eating establishment, the Barnstable Restaurant and Tavern, welcomed diners. Lucy decided she'd give it a try. The new restaurant had purchased pieces of furniture from the Barnstable

Lucy's little ghost now haunts this restaurant.

House, and Lucy hitched a ride. The child ghost became particularly fond of a young waitress. She tugged at the waitress's uniform, hoping to get her to play. But Lucy's timing was off, and the waitress finally told her that she had work to do, and she'd have to move on. Lucy's ghost has also been spotted skipping up the stairs of this historic 1799 structure, the former site of the Globe Hotel for more than a hundred years. A middle-aged resident of Barnstable confided that he had rented office space on the second floor and that several times he had seen a little girl with brown hair and wearing a blue dress waiting on the stair landing. She would grin at him, then turn and scamper down the hallway. If he tried to follow her, the tiny apparition would "fade away."

Susan's ghost lives at the Simmons Homestead.

10

Don't Let Susan Out

Bill Putman acts like an over-protective father when it comes to the little ghost girl who haunts the Simmons Homestead Inn in Hyannis Port. Putman worries that if she ran off, she wouldn't know what to do, and something might happen to her. It happened once before. "The first time Susan got out was in 1833, and she drowned in the pond. She was the daughter of Lemuel Simmons."

Sea captain Lemuel Baker Simmons and his family lived in the farmhouse that was built by his father, Sylvanus Simmons, around 1810. Lemuel and his wife, Temperance, had nine children, four girls and five boys. Temperance died in September of 1841. Five months later, in February 1842, Lemuel married a widow, Eliza Bearse, and they had two children, a girl and a boy. According to the 1850 Federal Census, all of these children were alive and living at the farmhouse, but little Susan is not listed. The twenty-acre pond where the seven-year-old child drowned stills exits and is now owned by the town.

Bill Putman and his wife, Suzy, had always intended to own and operate a country inn. "We felt it was a good way to retire." Sadly, Putman's wife died before their plan became a reality. "I didn't want to go back to the corporate world," says soft-spoken Putman, "and then this came on the market. I bought it in 1988 and have had it [ever since]. I did not believe in ghosts and had never seen a ghost until I came here." At the time of his purchase, the house had been a summer home for the Groves family. "It had no heat or anything like that." When Putman began his massive, one-man restoration, he discovered he had a little spirit to keep him company.

"When I first came here, I was painting walls and stuff like that. I was upstairs in the back hallway, and I sort of begin to see something out of the corner of my eye. I hear a giggle, and I see her duck around the corner. I have never experienced anything like that. She had long brown hair, wore a white dress, and was about four feet tall. I guess she was checking to see that I wasn't screwing up her daddy's house."

Initially, Putman did not have a name for his blithe spirit. A psychic who was staying in room number five, the Owl Room, came down to breakfast one morning and asked the innkeeper if he knew he had a ghost. Putman replied, "Yes, I do, but how did you know?" The woman informed him that "I was up all night talking to her, and she told me her name is Susan." After staying in the same room, other guests, unaware of little Susan's tragic death, have also sat down to breakfast and talked about having a strange sensation that they were sharing the room with "a presence." They described the presence as "friendly and happy."

The Owl Room may have been Susan's bedroom.

Putman describes Susan as a shy but curious ghost. When a female guest leaves the room, Susan will inspect her make-up. She'll uncap lipsticks, dip brushes in eye shadow, and open compacts. She does not tidy up after herself very well. Putman believes she does this on purpose, so that people will notice that she's around. "She likes attention, and she deserves all she can get."

Susan's "foster father" and protector worries about her. "As more and more people heard about our ghost, the ghost hunters started coming around, so I am careful who I let in because she deserves better than that. One ghost hunting couple tried to take photographs, and the next morning, they got up and the film had been rerolled—there was nothing on it." Putman smiles. "She got them."

The Simmons Homestead has ten guestrooms in the main house and an additional two in the attic, which have been used by staff. In the winter of 1991, Felicia Shea worked as the assistant innkeeper. She remembered going to her attic bedroom and finding the "drawers of my dresser were pulled open." Shea also noticed that a few of her personal items were out of place on her dressing table. Since no was else was staying in the main house at the time, Shea attributed the childish pranks to a small spirit who wanted to explore. To entertain her inquisitive ghost, the assistant innkeeper picked up a book from the nightstand and began to read out loud. "She read *Forever Amber* to her and started calling our ghost Amber," says Putman, who prefers Susan as a more appropriate choice of name. Shea continued her habit of reading to "Amber" whenever she felt her presence but switched to a more suitable selection of reading material—children's books borrowed from the local library. "I think Susan kept hanging out with Felicia because she thought of her as a big sister," considers Putman.

Putman believes that prior to her death, Susan would have played in the attic as a child, running back and forth with her sisters and brothers. He has also noticed over the years that Susan's tiny spirit seems to prefer female guests as her new playmates, with one exception, Putman's stepson, Craig. "He experienced a presence in the upstairs hallway near room five when he was thirteen years old."

Since room five is Susan's favorite in the afterlife, the assumption is that it might have been hers as a child.

Indeed, the current animal kingdom décor of the entire inn has built-in kid appeal. "It started with my wife; she did needlepoint wall hangings of birds. When I came down here, I didn't plan on making all the rooms have animal themes; it just sort of grew. The Elephant Room was the first, and well . . . damn thing now is completely out of control."

Guests have their choice of the Cat Suite, Dogs Room (there is a bulletin board where people can pin up pictures of their dogs), Rabbit Hutch Room, Geese with a Few Cows Room, Jungle Room, Fish Aquarium Room, or Birds, Butterflies, and Parrots Room. Susan's preferred haunt, room five, is the Owl Room. The adjacent annex houses the Cape Cod Critters and Little Critters Rooms and the Horse and Hound Suite.

The amiable host of the Simmons Homestead, a Yale graduate with a degree in geology and MBA in marketing from New York University, is now a self-professed animal addict. "I started putting

The Fish Aquarium Room, one of the themed bedrooms at the inn.

some critters around as decorations." These decorations peer from
shelves, preen on paintings, posture in needlepoint wall hangings,
and perch on bars suspended from the ceilings. "I can't abide empty
spaces," confesses the innkeeper.

Putman has made an attempt to tame the animal overload with
a link to the home's history. "Last winter, I kind of toned it down
a little. I converted the Giraffe Room into the Dog Room, and the
Elephant Room is the Atlantic Room because Lemuel Simmons was
the youngest sea captain to sail the seven seas." But Putman couldn't
help sneaking in a few animals when he redid the Zebra Room. "It's
now the Simmons Pond Room, so it has toads and little turtles."

With so many carved, enameled, appliquéd, sculpted, and stuffed
animals, it's not surprising that Putman is also a caretaker of the real
thing. At one time, he had thirty-three cats. Their names all start
with the letter A because "I want them all to feel like alpha cats." The
leaders of this feline menagerie are Abigail and her successors, Abigail
One and Abigail Too.

Astair (named after Fred) is the official greeter—he welcomes

Animals adorn every surface of the common room.

every guest on arrival, follows them around the grounds, and is the last furry face they see on departure. In deference to guests who have allergies, all of the cats are banned from the main house. However, Abigail tends to ignore the rules. While guests are encouraged to explore and enjoy the Simmons Homestead and all of the sights of nearby Hyannis, the laid-back innkeeper does have one very important rule. A sign on the front door warns: "DON'T LET ABIGAIL IN, OR SUSAN OUT."

Abigail is one very smart, persistent cat, who does her best to have guests break Putnam's rule. As for the second half of his commandment, a seven-year-old ghost child shouldn't be tempted to roam alone outside. As Putman is fond of saying, "We welcome and enjoy little Susan. After all, this has been her house a lot longer than it's been ours."

Lagniappe: Mixed in among the merry mishmash of animal artifacts

Astair (named after Fred), the official greeter.

at the Simmons Homestead on Scudder Avenue in Hyannis Port are antique beds, private baths with claw-foot tubs, lace curtains, Queen Anne chairs, and cozy fireplaces. "I wanted to create a space that feels like home," says the innkeeper, who refers to himself as "the purveyor of timely tiny tidbits of trivia." The relaxed atmosphere of the inn consistently earns rave reviews. During the 1991 Robert Kennedy Memorial golf tournament, the Kennedy family rented the entire inn for a slew of high-profile guests: Dinah Shore, Carly Simon, James Woods, and former Olympic gold medal decathlon winner Bruce Jenner.

The adjacent annex serves as an adult playhouse with billiards and a barroom, where Putman houses his single malt Scotch whisky collection, featuring well more than six hundred varieties from every distillery and region in Scotland. "The main reason, other than compulsion, is that I like single malts . . . I haven't had a cold in more than thirty years—seems like as good a reason as any to hoard them and drink them." The jovial host is more than willing to have tastings with his guests and would be happy to have the ghost of

Putman's single malt whisky collection.

Toad Hall houses antique cars.

Lemuel Simmons belly up to the bar, but he knows that's never going to happen. Simmons was an avowed teetotaler, and the captain sailed out of Boston Harbor on the first ship to *not* offer rum rations to its crew. That's okay with the present owner, who finds loving companionship with his feline menagerie that hangs out here on every available space.

Putman, a former race car driver, also collects sports cars and owns fifty-eight of them, all red. He owns vintage English Triumphs, Austin Healeys, Jaguars, and MGs. Most of them are stored in Toad Hall, a series of sheds between the main house and the annex. Putman explains his choice of the name for the antique car garage. "It's from *The Wind in the Willows.* Toad was the main character, and he was fascinated with the new motor cars of the late 1800s." Bill Putman loves them all: cars, cats, Scotch whisky, and Susan.

11

Must Love Ghosts

A disgruntled guest of the Colonial House Inn in Yarmouth Port complained that no one told her the inn was haunted. She insisted that a warning sign be posted out front: "MUST LOVE GHOSTS."

"We lasted only two nights due to the ghosts who bothered us . . . My husband saw this lady in white when we first arrived. . . . At three-thirty a.m. we were awakened by a blood-curdling scream. The next night, I left the light on all night and did not sleep one wink.

The haunted Colonial House Inn, where ghosts run rampant.

. . . I would never stay here again or recommend this inn to anyone unless they loved ghosts."

Owner Malcom Perna is unfazed. A translucent lady who tends to an invisible garden, a rocking chair that turns of its own volition to face a wall, a non-existent baby crying through the night—he simply adds the paranormal observations to his growing "Ghost Ledger." "I knew nothing about ghost stories associated with the property when I purchased it, and I couldn't have cared less." Now, keeping track of the ghostly apparitions and their favorite hot spots has become an entertaining sidebar to his duties as innkeeper.

"People started telling me about the ghosts here, so I started recording it. I would write the date, sometimes people's names, sometimes not, but what was more important was what was said and what area of the inn they were in when they saw or heard or did whatever this was. And [since 1979] I have been amazed; if the same type of story has happened or been reported to me in the same area—and it's a big property—it gives credence. To just hear that you got a voice somewhere in the inn doesn't mean a thing, but if I can connect it to a room or area where I have had a report before, then there is a credibility level. But if I can't, that's okay too."

Paranormal activities at the inn run the gamut. The apparitions— male or female, adults, teens, or babies—are all connected to previous occupants from several centuries of ownership. A portrait of a fearsome sea captain with a thick white beard hangs above the fireplace in the Oak Room, one of three dining areas on the first floor of the inn. Perna acknowledges the portrait with a quick nod. "This is Capt. Fay Parker, the last of about eleven sea captains who owned this house. This portrait was done in 1900." Adhering to his policy of letting each visitor encounter and/or identify a specific ghost based on their personal experience, Perna will not reveal if Captain Fay haunts the Oak Room. Instead, the innkeeper gives an overview of the history of the house, and, in the process, introduces a few of the likely contenders who have lived here and never left.

"Essentially, the house was built in the 1730s as a Federal-style two-story building with a hip roof. Originally built by the Josiah

Capt. Fay Parker stares down from his portrait in the Oak Room.

Ryder family, it was acquired by the Capt. Joseph Eldridge family, and they had sea captain after sea captain after sea captain." For the next one-hundred-plus years, the home was known as the Eldridge House. A Doric-columned portico altered the style of the front façade from Federal to Victorian. "They were making things grander. . . . You see, these sea captains weren't just sea captains . . . they were shipping magnets. By the time the 1850s came . . . these same two families, the Eldridges and the Thachers [relatives by marriage], had moved the center of operations to Boston, so this would have been their summer home."

Sadly, this grand summer home was the site of numerous deaths. Capt. Joseph Eldridge lived here as early as 1804. He and his wife had nine children; four died before reaching their first birthday. In his will, the captain left the house to his youngest child, Azariah. Dr. Azariah Eldridge and his wife, Ellen, had only one child, who died at a young age. Both Azariah and Ellen suffered from poor health.

When Azariah died in 1856, Ellen was too ill to attend the funeral. Having no heir, Ellen left the house to the First Congregational Church.

"Three hundred and fifty years . . . that is not unusual, childbirths and deaths," says Perna. What veers into the realm of the exceptional are the wails of sick babies echoing in one room of the inn. "That thing is consistent, and it is always the same part of the house. You hear a baby crying and there is no baby."

Another peculiar manifestation could be linked to the same poor babies and their worried mothers. In a bedroom in the main house a rocking chair has been found to turn itself around during the night and face the wall. "This is a reoccurring event," confirms the owner. Although the ability of an inanimate object to move at will defies logic, Perna knows it is also a case of the rocking chair being in the wrong position. "To be perfectly honest, I am familiar with the alterations made to the house. That blank wall the rocking chair turns to face used to have a window." The real debate seems to be whether the rocking chair possesses a supernatural ability or whether a mother's loving spirit turns the chair back to its original position so she can lull her colicky baby to sleep.

The Colonial House Inn has eleven guest rooms in the manor house and ten in the converted Carriage House. The Carriage House also has a two-story cupola. "Originally it was a small, single one, and then they built a top story to house a water tank. They used a windmill to pump the water up there, and gravity feeds the water throughout the complex." Perna boasts that the Eldridges had "indoor plumbing before there was such a thing: this is called having money." These sea captains also employed stable boys to care for their horses and carriage. One forlorn lad took his own life.

"I do know that a young, sixteen-year-old boy committed suicide here inside the carriage house. He hung himself." The innkeeper conducted an extensive background check. "I have studied the archives of the *Register* newspaper about the events that have occurred. I am past president of the historical society, so obviously a real history of this house, not a paranormal history of the house, is

A young boy hung himself in the carriage house.

very important to me." Nevertheless, Perna meticulously records each and every account claiming to hear the voice of a young boy crying in the carriage house along with reported sounds of horses neighing. With the exception of native wildlife, only well-behaved pets (limited to dogs and cats) are permitted at the inn.

Elizabeth Embler, whose parents rented out rooms during the summer season, remembers an encounter with another ghostly presence. In the slow winter season, she had her pick of bedrooms. However, room number eight proved to be a poor choice. She awoke at night to find a stranger moving about her room. At first she was not afraid, thinking it might be a guest who had mistaken her room for theirs (it had happened before). But that time, it was different. Embler instinctively knew the figure was "not a real person." In her account to the Yarmouth Historical Society, Embler relates that the male presence was facing away with his arms folded. She watched apprehensively as he looked at one window and then turned to look out another. He was dressed in clothes of "a different generation." The phantom lingered for ten minutes and then vanished. Embler was unable to positively identify him as one of the many sea captains who lived in the house because "he was more like a shadow."

The "translucent lady in white" is another reoccurring apparition, only she haunts the grounds, not the house itself. "A lady dressed in period clothes is working in what appears to be a garden." Perna speaks in riddles. "Somewhere in the middle of an open space, she's out there in a garden that is not really a garden, but may have been a garden, not one of the gardens you see now."

The innkeeper's arms are folded across his chest. He is in the tavern, a warm inviting space just off the lobby. A black-and-white sketch of the mansion as it appeared during the 1880s looms over his shoulder. "I don't know who she was, but I know there was a garden here almost two hundred years ago, and I happen to know where." Perna turns to face the framed image of the house with its extensive front lawn, young trees, and pathways. What seems to be a glass greenhouse (no longer in existence) is to the right. Perna taps the image gently with his finger. "So, when you talk about seeing a ghost gardening in an open space, that's how I can tell whether there is validity to your story or not. Remember, I am a historian."

Many of the haunted tales associated with the inn are well known. The innkeeper has developed his own methods for ensuring that the reports from his guests are not merely a repeat of haunted tales already in circulation: he runs his version of a double-blind study.

He refuses to divulge the specific rooms where alleged hauntings have occurred. "I never say room numbers, and all the numbers [of the haunted rooms] you hear about have probably been changed. If you go online you are going to read something about room 224. There is no room number 224, but I do this intentionally." Perna doesn't want to sway or influence a guest's perception of what might happen. "I don't want to say to you, 'You are staying in room 7, and what has been reported in room 7 is that after midnight the closet door just keeps opening and closing.' And then you'll be

Malcom Perna will neither confirm nor deny which rooms are haunted.

thinking about that, and the next morning you are going to come down and say, 'Guess what, Mac? That damn door kept me awake all night!'" For Perna, when this happens, "There is no validity to what you are telling me." On the other hand, explains the innkeeper, "If you come down and say, 'You know, I was in room 7 last night— or 107 or 207—and the damn door kept opening or closing,' and there was no wind that night, I record it and look back and I see that four years before that someone else shared the same story." The innkeeper sees the needle on the plausibility factor rise a few degrees.

To deter other guests from assuming that just because there is a rocking chair in the room it is *the* rocking chair, Perna flooded the inn with them. "I have since put eight rocking chairs in various rooms and turned them all around to face the windows. Otherwise, it's out there on the internet so everyone is talking about it, and if you stay in a room with a rocking chair, you'll be convinced you saw something that didn't happen." Only Perna knows which one is the real "haunted rocking chair."

The supernatural buzz surrounding the Colonial House Inn naturally attracted the ghost hunters. "We have been investigated by paranormal groups over twenty times." With a sly smile Pena adds, "No one ever leaves those investigations empty handed."

In 2006, the Spirit Encounters Research Team (SERT), arrived ready to go to work. Prior to their arrival, Perna took down all pictures and documents that might offer clues. At the conclusion of their investigation, medium Richard Boisvere made his report to Perna. "At no time did I or any member of my team feel threatened in any way. All experiences were playful, mischievous and/or friendly. Team members experienced sensations of being touched near the dance floor . . . EVPs [Electronic Voice Phenomenon] near the Widow's Watch recorded children's voices, and the sound of footsteps running up and down stairs. A recording made at 1:45 a.m. had a child's voice whispering 'Hello.'"

CAPS, the Cape and Island Paranormal Society, also published findings on their Web site of the Colonial House Inn, which included sightings of apparitions, sounds, and moving objects. Perna says he

As part of his blind study, Perna has flooded the house with rocking chairs.

did not make them privy to any specifics. "I just let them do their thing. I told them, 'If you guys want to find something, go find it.'" The innkeeper notes that what these groups have reported during their investigations have "matched what I have in my ledger many times. Almost always they come up with at least one match without my helping them."

Each year at Halloween, Perna hosts "Ghost Hunting 101" and invites a different paranormal group for the weekend affair. "It starts off with a cocktail party in the afternoon in which a paranormal group shows you the equipment, teaches you how to use it . . . and sets up the equipment to run overnight. On Saturday evening . . . you review what the equipment might have captured. Guests love it. It's the best entertainment in the world."

Malcom Perna is quite clear when it comes to his personal beliefs. "I don't feel it's my duty to prove one way or another that the inn is haunted." He pauses to let the impact of his statement settle in before continuing. "My favorite thing to say is that I have never seen a ghost! And if I ever did, he or she (the ghost) would have two choices: pay for the room for the night or do some work. Maybe that's why I have never seen a ghost."

Lagniappe: When Malcom Perna purchased the property in 1979, "It was deserted, deteriorated." However, it did meet some of his other criteria. "It had to be a *significant* home. I wanted a property that I could develop into an inn, and it had to have lawns and gardens." Along with restoring and enlarging the main house, Perna created tranquil garden spaces. The innkeeper waves his arm in the direction of the triangular-shaped Yarmouth Port Village Green. "At one time, the Eldridges and the Thachers owned all the property around here, but what people did when a son or daughter was getting married, is they said, 'Okay, we'll take a plot of this land and we'll build a house for you next door.'"

The Edward Gorey House is a prime example. "When one of the Thachers who owned this house gave parcels of his property to his two daughters, it wound up that the back of the second daughter's

Edward Gorey's home of the last eleven years of his life.

barn was actually on her father's property, but it didn't matter because it was all in the family." "Technically," says a complacent Perna, "the [Edward Gorey House] barn is on my property by about four or five inches. Who cares? It's done now."

Edward Gorey, the Tony award-winning set designer for the Broadway hit *Dracula,* was a good neighbor, who lived around the corner from the Colonial House Inn for the last fourteen years of his life. In a March 2011, *New York Times* "News Bulletin from the Spirit World" reporter Mark Dery wrote, "The specter of Edward Gorey . . . is haunting our collective unconscious . . . His poisonously funny little picture books, deadpan accounts of murder, disaster and discreet depravity . . . established him as the master of high-camp macabre." A tour of the Edward Gorey House is the perfect paranormal follow-up to the specters at the Colonial House Inn.

A window display at the Edward Gorey House.

Skulls and skeletons, doorknobs and rocks, bats, ravens, and a tiny Amy doll caught mid-fall on the stairs are all part of the helter-skelter ambiance of Edward Gorey's world, in which "more is happening out there than we are aware of."

The Old Yarmouth Inn in Brewster.

12

Who Let the Dogs Out?

Established in 1696, the Old Yarmouth Inn lays claim to being the oldest inn on Cape Cod. Situated at the halfway point between Plymouth and Provincetown, it was a welcome stagecoach stop for weary travelers seeking lodging, food, and drink. Sheila FitzGerald and Arpad Voros, the present owners, are convinced that a good number of these old souls are still out and about.

FitzGerald, a vivacious and energetic host, is excited to introduce their ghosts. "Our main ghost, his name is Bradford Powell. He owned this place back in the late 1800s/early 1900s. He was a dentist, and he ran his dental practice downstairs and lived with his family upstairs. Anyone one who has seen our ghost describes him as a man about five foot eight [inches], rotund, with a giant crown of hair and huge jowls. That's how I saw him at Thanksgiving." She inhales and rushes on: "I was at the host stand, and someone had left the front door open. I was thinking 'I should close that,' and as I was standing there, the ghost walked by me. He was wearing a wool suit, French cuff sleeves, black boots, and he had this fluffy crown of hair." FitzGerald pivots her head from side to side. "And I was like, 'Anybody? Anybody?' hoping someone else was seeing what I was seeing. It was very cool. That was the first time I had actually seen the ghost."

But it was not the first time Bradford Powell had been spotted in the restaurant.

FitzGerald stands by a strangely shaped wooden sign in the lobby. Three weathered boards are banded in iron, and the bottom curves and hooks to the right. The sign reads: "Yarmouth Inn." Towards

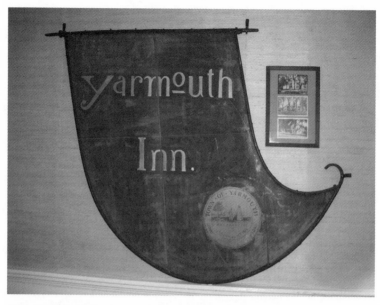

The sign attracted a ghost.

The sign features a seal that reads, in part, "Mattacheese Incorporated 1639."

the bottom is a round seal proclaiming the Town of Yarmouth and featuring a distinguished-looking Indian with a single feather headdress in front of a teepee. A sailboat is in the distance. Beneath these figures are the words: "Mattacheese Incorporated 1639" (Mattacheese is an alternate spelling for Metachee, a Wampanoag Native American village).

A friend had alerted FitzGerald that the sign was being sold at an upcoming auction. The restaurateurs immediately purchased it. "When we got it back, it was really exciting for us." Hanging to the right of the sign are three early photos of the inn. In the top photo, the outline of the hooked sign is discernible. "Originally, we had the sign in the Red Room near the fireplace. It generated a lot of interest." A curious ghost soon arrived to check it out.

"Around closing time, shortly after we got the sign, Keri, our server/bartender, and my bus boy were here—no one else. So Keri goes to the front door to lock up and passes the Red Room and there is a guy staring at the sign. And she's like 'What?' She backs away, and then he disappeared."

The owner enters the small, tastefully decorated foyer and pulls open the drawer of an antique sideboard. She rummages through a pile of photographs until she locates a yellowed and faded photo of a large man in a fisherman's sweater sitting on a rock on the beach. His arm is around a slender teenage girl. "See, here is Bradford; he is bald with just a ring of long hair sticking up on top of his head. He is sitting with his granddaughter Althea. She gave us this photo." FitzGerald says that before they had the photo to confirm the identity of their ghost, people would always describe the male apparition in the same way. "The first reported sighting of our ghost was by Carleton Davis, who was the artistic director for the Cape Playhouse, and he was staying upstairs when this was an inn. It was about four a.m. He woke to find a gentleman staring at him, a puzzled look on his face. He described in detail what he saw, right down to Bradford's jowls and crown of white hair."

When Bradford's granddaughter Althea Davis shared the photo of her grandfather, she also confirmed some of the gossip and rumors

Bradford Powell with his granddaughter Althea. (Photograph courtesy Sheila FitzGerald)

about her philandering relative. "Althea was still alive—she was ninety-eight when we when we took over." It was from Althea that Sheila FitzGerald and Arpad Voros first heard about Bradford's mistress and her tragic end.

Besides his dental practice, Bradford ran a second business out of the house. "He used the spare rooms as a boarding house for the teachers for the one-room schoolhouse up the street, which is now the fire station" At night, after his family was asleep, Bradford would sneak up the back staircase to see his mistress, who just happened to be the schoolteacher in residence.

In the reception area of the inn (which operates today solely as a restaurant), the huge wood-burning fireplace warms the room. "This is not a central fireplace. If you look here, this fireplace and the two fireplaces on either side, they mirror each other upstairs as well. Althea accidentally discovered the secret room built between the fireplaces.

When she was a young girl, she was playing and opened a bunch of closets and fell down behind the chimney. She screamed for help. One of the teachers heard her, followed the screams, and discovered she had fallen into this secret room that existed behind the fireplace."

Althea never revealed if the secret room was used by her grandfather for his clandestine affair, or if the teacher who came to her rescue was also her grandfather's mistress. What is known is that the mistress/schoolteacher later died in the house; smoke inhalation from the wood-burning fireplace is the prevailing theory behind her mysterious death.

FitzGerald believes that Bradford's mistress is the ghost who haunts the second floor. "She is not nearly as nice as Bradford. She's like the scary ghost. She's more of a troublemaker and a bit of a bigot. I call her a bigot because when I had my friends here from the British Virgin Islands, she was very, very, mean. We all had cocktails and were having a fun time for ourselves until we were so exhausted, we finally went to bed."

Althea accidentally discovered the secret room wedged between the fireplaces.

In the morning, FitzGerald was surprised to find her friend Michael Blaize sitting on the deck with his suitcase packed. "I asked him if everything was okay; 'You're not leaving until tomorrow.' He looked at me and said, 'I'm not spending another night here.' Naturally, I asked him why." Michael's reply stunned both FitzGerald and Voros, who had joined them on the deck. Their guest was adamant that he had to leave because he refused to be tormented again. "I am lying in bed last night, and I felt somebody was sitting on the bed next to me and there was nobody there, so I pulled the covers up over my head, hoping I was dreaming. The next thing I know, somebody is tickling my feet. So I open up my eyes—and there is nobody there. So I covered myself up and said if one more thing happens, I'm leaving. And then . . . somebody grabbed the posts on the bed and started shaking it hard, banging it on the floor."

"I am having a hard time believing a word Michael is saying. I am thinking he had a bad dream. Arpad and I exchanged glances," recalls FitzGerald. "However, Voros's ninety-three-year-old mother was living with us at the time," explains FitzGerald. "She comes out on the porch and we greet her, 'Hi Grandma.' She's not happy. She keeps saying, 'No good, no good.' I ask, 'Ma, what's the matter?' She goes, 'These boys no good.' I ask her again, 'What do you mean?' She says, 'These boys all night long, banging, banging, banging.'" FitzGerald raises her eyebrows. "I'm like, okay. Michael was right; the ghost got in his room."

Both owners are happy that the female ghost "does not interact with the guests and staff as much as Bradford does," although they do question the reason behind some of the stranger ghostly antics. "Our waiter David was waiting on someone in the Red Room. They were at the corner table near the stove (we added the stove to the front of the fireplace because it's more efficient). The couple had paid their bill, and David went to give them their change. He opened his hand and a quarter fell out. It did one of those rolling things, and it landed in front of the stove. He bent down to pick it up, and it got sucked right under the stove into the fireplace. Crazy!"

FitzGerald ticks off one incident after another. "My sister Maureen,

A quarter was mysteriously sucked up under the stove in the Red Room.

back in the early days, was staying with us. She was building a house and it wasn't ready. We would get up every morning and go for a walk, and she would go down to make the coffee because we walked the first half-mile with a coffee cup in our hands. This particular morning, she goes down to make the coffee, and all of a sudden the Hobart mixer started going on its own. That was it. She ran upstairs and yelled out, 'The mixer is going! The mixer is going!' Scared her to death."

No room is spared from ghostly hijinks. "Another time, we were sitting in the tavern at this table right here." FitzGerald indicates a square table between two windows. "My sister was with her then-husband, Christopher, and we were having dinner. It was late around nine o'clock, and then this sounds starts—*Whoowhoowhoowhoowhoo*. FitzGerald makes a face. "Christopher was famous for doing that thing with a glass where you wet your finger and run it around the rim and it makes that sound. And I am looking at him, and he says,

'My hands are right here.' I see he's got both hands flat on the table, but I still don't believe that he didn't do it. So I'm sitting across from him and glaring at him, and all of a sudden that whole window just shook, from the window sill all the way up, just howled.

"Another night, Judy, my bartender, was making drinks in the tavern, and she kept putting a glass down and it kept sliding back towards her. And she's like 'Sheila, Sheila,' and I said, 'It's probably just has some ice on it.' So she wiped the glass and the bar top down, and the glass kept sliding towards her so finally she just took the drink and put it over at the other end of the bar. When she did that the dividers between the window panes just flew off the window and hit the bar." FitzGerald slams her hand against the front of the wooden bar, imitating the force of the impact. "Judy went running out, white as a ghost."

Back in the main dining room, FitzGerald speaks of a more recent occurrence. "We don't have any candles in this house. We use

An unseen hand slid a glass across the bar.

A haunted window in the dining room.

rechargeable inserts that look like candles because they're user friendly and safer. Sunday morning, I came here and I noticed candle wax. I asked Andrew, one of our managers, 'Who was burning a candle last night?' He said, 'Nobody. Why?' I asked him again, 'Really, there was nobody here lighting candles?' Andrew insisted, 'We barely used the dining room last night.' I pointed out the candle wax on the white table cloth. It left a trail down the tablecloth and all the way across the rug, as if someone had been holding a candle and took a walk across the room." FitzGerald repeats, "We have no burnable candles anywhere in this restaurant."

Sheila FitzGerald saves the most mystifying tale for the grand, ghostly climax. "Oh, I have the best story—it's awesome, and it took place upstairs, so it could have been the female ghost, the mistress. And I have it on video, so we have proof!" She shows off pictures of two long-haired black dogs. "Wheezie and Indi [Indiana] are both rescues; Wheezie is a basset hound and lab, and Indi is a lab hound. They stay upstairs. Wheezie is an amazing watchdog. You can't open the door without her barking and carrying on.

"It was April of [2012]. We only live right across the street, but we drive the dogs back and forth. We don't want them to know that Route 6A is the bridge between the two because we don't want them to get hurt. At about 8:30 that night, Arpad said, 'It's time to pack up the dogs.' I said, 'Okay.' I stopped to talk to Danny at the bar and I felt a cold draft and I thought, 'Oh, Arpad must have the dogs already,' and I ran upstairs. So I go upstairs and see that the dogs are outside on the deck. I thought, 'That's strange—they don't have their leashes on, and the door was ajar.' I opened it all the way, and then called them inside. They came right in when I called them. I put their leashes on and shut the door."

FitzGerald says she then stopped at the restroom, and as she was coming out, her husband came up the back stairs after moving the car around to load the dogs. Their conversation bounces back and forth as each tries to understand who let the dogs out.

When Voros asks FitzGerald when she opened the door, a confused FitzGerald responds, "Just now. What are you talking about?" She assumed it was her husband who had left the dogs unattended on the deck. "I got up here and the dogs were outside. I let them in."

Voros knows he didn't let them out. Alarms go off inside his head. If it wasn't his wife, they need to find out who has been sneaking around upstairs. "Check the security cameras."

A nervous FitzGerald instantly agrees.

The security tapes are timed stamped. FitzGerald hits rewind and reviews the footage. "At 7:31, Indiana comes down the hall. She had been sleeping at the top of the steps. And she stands at the outside door [leading to the upper deck], does like a play bow and stands up. The door is closed. For no reason at all that I can see, she turns around, looks up and starts wagging her tail at the wall. She does another play bow and walks down the hall. Six minutes later she comes running down the hall as if somebody has called her and runs straight outside."

FitzGerald's voice rises in amazement as she describes what is on the tape. "The door just opened for her. Twelve seconds later, Wheezie comes running down the hall and goes outside." FitzGerald holds up her hand palm out, as if she is taking an oath. "Now I promise you, if somebody had tried to open that door, the first dog you are going to see is Wheezie come with teeth snarling. Somehow the unseen *thing* in the wall communicated to the dogs, and they went outside, and I have it on video. I showed it to our guy who actually hooked up our cameras. He is a skeptic; he doesn't believe in anything. I replay the tape for him and his jaw dropped. He knows our dogs, and he will call me and ask before he comes over because he will not come over if they are here. He knows Wheezie will bark and bark." Fitzgerald quickly adds, "She is never going to bite anybody, but her bark is horrifying." The owner cannot contain her excitement. "It is the greatest story ever. The dog was holding his head up as if somebody was talking to him, you know, 'You go lay down,' and the next thing you know the door is open, and the door just doesn't open, we keep it locked. It is the best witnessed story that I have. It is crazy."

The restaurant's phone is ringing, and Voros comes in to take the call. Sheila FitzGerald's mind is still on who let the dogs out. "It could be Bradford. He's nice. He's not mean. He wouldn't let the dogs out thinking they would run away." She calls over to Voros and a discussion ensues, as if debating which ghost does what is a normal topic for everyday conversation.

"Who do you think opened the door, the woman or the man?" quizzes FitzGerald.

Voros considers the options and rules out Branford as the culprit. "The guy was really gentle."

"He's always gentle. He's sort of like the caretaker."

Voros agrees. "He's just here."

"I think it was her. The meanie. If it was the woman do you think she was letting the dogs out to be cruel, or to be helpful?"

"I just have no idea why that happened."

FitzGerald sums it up with a single word: supernatural.

Sheila FitzGerald attributes part of the reason for the on-going paranormal episodes to the fact that they "took [the building] over in

The Old Yarmouth Inn, a former stagecoach stop.

1996 on the tercentennial of this building's existence, and maybe we stirred things up."

Revealing that your restaurant is haunted might not be some entrepreneurs' idea of good marketing strategy, but FitzGerald has no such qualms. "It's fun. I love the fact that it has spirits—it makes the Old Yarmouth Inn such a unique place. We assume our ghosts are Bradford Powell and his mistress. They both died here, but who knows who else might still be around. History doesn't really tell you how many people have passed through."

Lagniappe: The Old Yarmouth Inn's guest registry from the 1860s records the names of hundreds of travelers who found respite here. Prior to its establishment as a colonial town, the land near Yarmouth was home to the Native American village of Metachee. According to genealogical researchers, in 1639 Englishman Austin Bearse married Mary "Little Dove" Hyanno in a Wampanoag tribal ceremony, which critics of the time disparagingly referred to as a "pagan" ritual. Mary was the daughter of sachem (chief) John Iyanough of the Cummaquid, granddaughter of Highyanough, sachem of the Wampanoag, and great-granddaughter of Canonicus, chief of the Narragansett. The union of Mary and Austin became a major factor in the temporary peace that existed for more than two generations between the Wampanoag and the English on Cape Cod. At the same time, the marriage merged Christian tradition with the Native American belief in the spirit world: the spirit of a deceased person never dies but simply moves to another place, and communication between these worlds is always possible.

The proliferation of haunted tales in the town of Yarmouth, incorporated in 1793, can also be traced to the influence of religious dogma on the local citizenry. Just up the street from the Old Yarmouth Inn, the Church of New Jerusalem followed the philosophy of eighteenth-century Christian mystic Emanuel Swedenborg, who claimed to have an ability to commune with the dead. During a profound religious crisis, Swedenborg went into a trance where he spoke with angels, Jesus, devils, and departed human souls.

Followers of mystic Emanuel Swedenborg worshipped here.

During the colonial era, it was common to build taverns close to churches. After long hours in unheated houses of worship, parishioners sought the warm hearth of the local tavern, imbibing liquid refreshments while feasting on hearty fare. The current restaurant honors the centuries-old tradition with a Sunday brunch buffet, "a slightly decadent indulgence." As they updated and modernized the Old Yarmouth Inn Sheila FitzGerald and Arpad Voros worried that their improvements might have a negative impact on their resident spirits. "We were afraid after we did the renovation six years ago, we weren't going to see any ghosts after that."

Bradford Powell, his mistress, and the other as-yet-unnamed souls have alleviated the owners' concerns by maintaining an active presence both upstairs and down at the Old Yarmouth Inn.

The Scargo Café, home to the ghost of Luther Hall.

13

A Haunted Café, a Legend, and a Lake

Brothers David and Peter Troutman opened the Scargo Café in 1987. Their intent was to succeed where five previous restaurants had failed, among those a Finnish smörgåsbord and Mrs. O'Leary's Milk Bar. Approaching the three-decade mark, the popularity of the Scargo Café in Dennis Village is due to the Troutman brothers' emphasis on service and attention to detail. What they hadn't factored in were a pair of ghosts.

In their first three years of operation, an aggressive spirit made all who worked there uncomfortable. The first floor of the sprawling building on Main Street has four cozy, wood-paneled dining rooms and an outdoor wrap-around deck. The second floor is used as a business office, storage space, and a changing room for staff. Within weeks of opening, it became apparent that the wait staff preferred to put on their uniforms in the restrooms on the first floor. The objections to the designated second-floor changing room ranged from "it feels creepy up there" to more specific complaints about being "poked in the back by bony fingers." One male waiter swore that when he went upstairs to get an extra highchair from the storage area, the belligerent presence attacked him. The waiter felt two hands on his back followed by a hard shove, nearly propelling him and the highchair down the stairs. When the waiter regained his balance, he turned around, but the angry spirit had vanished. Less frightening incidents—an unsettling sense of being watched, heavy breathing with no one there—continued from 1987 to 1990 and then abruptly stopped. It seems the malevolent ghost hitched a ride.

The Scargo Café employs a year-round staff of fifty food service professionals, which increases by another twenty during the busy summer months. The seasonal workers are often college students. After her summer employment ended, a particularly congenial college-bound student stopped in to say her goodbyes and wish everyone well. As she got into her car and turned on to the Mid-Cape Highway, she had an uneasy sense that she was not alone. After she checked into her dorm, she called a close friend on staff at the café and confided that something peculiar happened on her trip. Owner David Troutman confirms the story. "She said that the ghost from the café had been in her car. It felt like there was something bad in her backseat. When she got to the Sagamore Bridge leading off the Cape, it was as if the ghost—the 'bad thing'—didn't want to cross the canal. She thought the ghost jumped out into the water because once she crossed over she wasn't frightened by his presence anymore." When questioned why he thought a ghost would hitch a ride with the former waitress, Troutman, impeccably attired in a gray pin-striped suit, briefly ponders his reply and then grins, "She was young and pretty, why not?"

Troutman further speculates that the ghost might have been the troubled spirit of a very disturbed young man known as Junior who lived in the building in the 1950s when it was still a private residence.

Fortunately for the Troutman brothers, their second ghost causes only minor disruptions: lights pop on and off; silverware disappears from one table, then reappears on another; phones ring with no one on the other end; and an uncomfortable chill fills the air in front of the roaring fireplace in the lobby—all subtle yet manageable ghostly manifestations. The brothers would like to think that these are the calling cards of the spirit of Luther Hall, who built his home on the site in 1868. A faded photo of Luther, standing tall and proud in his dress-blue Civil War uniform, hangs in the hallway. At age eighteen, Luther enrolled as a clerk in Company E, Fifth Massachusetts regiment. Following a reenlistment, he was commissioned a captain of militia. After the Civil War, Luther embarked on a series of wide-ranging career choices. He began his civilian career as a clerk in the Howes Chapman candy store. Luther must have done very well because, in 1868, he built a spacious home on the site of the Scargo Café. In 1869, he married his boss's daughter Minerva Chapman. Gradually, Luther took over management of his father-in-law's store and operated it for twenty-five years until 1885. He also served as the village postmaster. He then "retired" and went into the cranberry business. Still seeking new challenges, he became an agent for the Nobscussett Hotel and later added chairman of the Dennis School System to his varied résumé. Luther Hall died on April 29, 1900, at the age of fifty-eight, but his fidgety spirit continues his ever-evolving pursuits, checking up on the operations of the Scargo Café in his former home.

Having lived in Dennis all of his life, Luther likely approves of the name of the restaurant. David Troutman explains the choice: "It was the legend of Princess Scargo and the lake. We wanted to honor and pay tribute to the village and its history." Scargo Lake is less than a mile down the road. The legend predates the arrival of the first white settlers.

It was the hot, dry summer of 1600, and the Nobscussett Indians lived frugally in a small encampment of barely one hundred people. Mashantam, the sachem (chief), had no sons and only one daughter. Princess Scargo possessed, it was said, an almost luminescent beauty, with eyes as radiant as the stars and hair as black as the night with no moon. A warrior arrived at the Nobscussett village and saw Scargo drawing water from the spring. The warrior threw back his shoulders and announced with fierce pride, "I am called Weaquaquet. I live many running days away." The two young people were instantly attracted to each other, but Weaquaquet could not stay; he had been sent by the great chief Massasoit to deliver a message of peace to all the villages of the mighty Wampanoag Nation. Weaquaquet promised Princess Scargo and her father that he would return and make her his bride. As proof of his love he would send a magical gift that had no equal in all the land.

In less than one sun, two braves arrived carrying an enormous pumpkin, so large that their legs trembled under the weight. The hollowed out pumpkin was filled with water. Swimming within were four shimmering fish. Princess Scargo made a solemn pledge to keep the little creatures alive as a sign of her growing love for Weaquaquet. Soon the fish were too big for their pumpkin home, and Scargo released them into the spring. Two died under the dwindling water and hot sun. The blistering heat continued, and the spring began to dry up. Scargo feared for the surviving fish. She wept and appealed to her father.

Mashantam stood on a rock above the spring and spoke to the people. "My daughter is crying. She weeps for Weaquaquet. She weeps for her fish that are dying. She weeps for her people, the Nobscussett who will soon have no water." Mashantam had a plan. He ordered his most skilled bowman to shoot an arrow as far away from the edge of the spring as he could. Where the arrow landed would be the other end of a new lake; here the tribe would grow and thrive. The Nobscussetts began to question their chief: "How will this be done? Where will we get water to fill this lake?" The sachem replied that everyone in the tribe would dig with clamshells and that Scargo's tears would fill the lake with water as blue and clear as the sky.

The men, women, and children of the Nobscussett tribe dug their lake in the shape of a fish and named it in honor of Princess Scargo, whose tears poured out to swell the lake with cool water. The fish multiplied, and there was food for all. Weaquaquet returned and reunited with his princess. The couple lived on the shores of Scargo Lake and had many children. Love has been said to move mountains—in this enduring legend, love carved a lake.

Dennis resident and former MIT rocket scientist Hugh Blair-Smith remembers hearing the legend from both his mother and his grandmother. There is a sad twist and a little bit of magic in their family's version: Princess Scargo receives from Weaquaquet just one fish, which will grow as long as the warrior is successful. When the fish outgrows the pumpkin, Scargo has her handmaidens weave a large, waterproof basket, and then a yet larger one, until the fish becomes too big for any basket. She then sets her handmaidens to work digging a pond in the shape of a fish, using mussel shells and

Scargo Lake, fashioned in the shape of a fish.

creating Scargo Hill. It is too late—the fish dies, and Princess Scargo's heart is broken because Weaquaquet will never return. Mashantam, the sachem and father of the distraught princess, orders his people to complete the lake. His daughter sits on the great hill, and her copious tears fill the lake. However, unlike ordinary mortals, the princess's tears are not salty; Scargo Lake is a fresh-water pond. Hugh Blair-Smith, like his great-uncle and great-great uncle before him, named his forty-five-foot sailing vessel, the *Mashantam*, in honor of the wise Nobscussett sachem who fashioned a lake in the shape of a fish.

For restaurateurs David and Peter Troutman, legends in all their varied forms are to be treasured. They are the enduring memories of those who walked the sandy shores of Cape Cod long before them.

Lagniappe: The best view of Scargo Lake is from Scargo Tower. Take Old Bass River Road to Scargo Hill Road. At the top of the hill, a thirty-foot, weathered, cobblestone turret rises like the ruins

Scargo Tower overlooks a legendary lake.

of some long-forgotten castle. Built in 1901, it replaced the original wooden tower first built by the Tobey family in 1874. It is open and free to the public. Climb the spiral staircase, and, on reaching the open space at the top, you will be at the highest point in the mid-Cape area. A mist rises from Cape Cod Bay, and beyond the bay, the Cape coastline, stretching to the tip of Provincetown, beckons in pastel hues of blues, browns, greens, and golden yellows. Directly below, Scargo Lake appears, as it was when it was first created, in the shape of a fish. Scientists describe it as a kettle pond formed by retreating glaciers or draining floodwaters, but folklore dismisses such technicalities. Scargo Hill, the only such hill next to a lake on the Cape, is the dirt scooped out by hand when the lake was dug. For a closer view, climb back down the tower and follow the path to Princess Beach. Dip your fingers in the clear water. See the fish swimming below the surface, and let your imagination drift back to a time when a beautiful young Native American woman received a token of love from her handsome warrior.

The Bramble Inn in Brewster.

14

Paranormal Fan Club

Ghosts don't haunt us. That's not how it works. They're present among us because we won't let them go.

—Sue Grafton, *M Is for Malice*

Like the Pied Piper of legend, spirits follow Ruth Manchester no matter where she goes. This award-winning chef offers a simple rationale for her thriving paranormal fan base. "I think it is like people who end up with stray cats—if there is a presence that is lost, [and] if you are at all receptive to that, they will find you. They need to find you, so if they are there, they make themselves known."

Ghost encounters tend to be one on one. For Ruth and her husband, Cliff, the spirits arrived en masse. "We lived in Brewster in a fairly new home but in an old, wooded area near a lake. It was right when we started negotiating to buy the Bramble Inn, which was in the fall of 1984, and we started having what we both call a visitation. It was a group of people. They would stand around our bed, which would put a damper on our romantic life for a while." While Ruth laughs about their unusual predicament, she admits that this initial exposure to ghosts had more than one drawback. "The room took on kind of a musty odor. It was cold during these visitations. Really, it was kind of creepy."

The visitations continued for several months. "We would hear a neighbor's dog barking—Sammy—across the street. He would start barking late at night. We would get into bed, and all of a sudden, these visions would come in. We had three cats at the time, and they used to come in, and they would take turns sleeping with us or one of my daughters, but when the visitations started, all the cats immediately stopped coming into our room."

Although most of the nocturnal intruders stayed in the shadows, one stood out. "The predominant person was someone that we called 'Ponce de León' because he had on one of those funny metal helmets. He had a goatee type of beard, and if you look at a picture of the Spanish explorer Ponce de León, he kind of looked like that."

Ruth and Cliff Manchester made no effort to dispel the spirits. "We didn't feel threatened; we just felt sadness, like they didn't want us to leave. They liked us—they were happy to see a happy family with three small children. It was just a sadness that they were conveying to us."

The Manchesters made the move to the Bramble Inn on Route 6A in Brewster at the beginning of 1985. "When we left, we never thought too much more about it except for saying to ourselves, 'Oh, isn't it nice to be able to sleep at night.'"

Two years later, in 1987, the Manchesters purchased Pepper House for additional guest accommodations and made an astonishing discovery. "We started doing renovations at the Pepper House, and there was an old-fashioned kitchen sink, which my husband pulled out because we were going to redo the kitchen. The flooring underneath had plywood boards that didn't match up with the pine boards, and when he ripped up the plywood, he noticed something a little shiny hidden underneath." Ruth pauses, not for dramatic effect, but because after all this time it is still hard to process the near-impossible coincidence. "It was a sterling silver ring with a square, carved, lapis face—the face of Ponce de León, our ghost." Ruth wraps up her true tale with a justifiable celebratory flair. "And when Cliff found the ring, he brought it over and showed it to me, and put it on my finger—and of course, it fit perfectly!"

By the early 1990s, Ruth and Cliff had three bed and breakfast establishments up and running in Brewster: the Bramble Inn, the Pepper House, and the 1849 House. Ruth's reputation as a master chef was growing, as was the occurrence of ghostly manifestations.

"At the 1849 House, we were redecorating. I was making

new curtains for the upstairs two-room suite. Everybody always complained about a presence, definitely not happy, there. Even the housekeeping staff would really run through and clean it as quickly as they could because they didn't want to be there." Ruth says that when she went over to the 1849 House to install the curtains, she was forced to deal with the unruly spirit. "I came upstairs and the radio just came on, and I thought someone had left the alarm on—the previous guest—but that wasn't the case: I checked, and the alarm hadn't been set. So, I turned it [the radio] off, and when I did, the door down downstairs leading to the front door slammed, and every hair on my body stood up." Ruth decided that her only recourse was to take charge of the situation. "I just started talking to this presence and I told him, 'I am not here in any threatening manner. All I want to do here is to change these curtains, so please let me do this.'" The ghostly reaction was instant. "All of a sudden, everything just quieted down, the air became breathable again, and he became reasonable again. I hung the curtains and left." Ruth did not have to admonish this ghost again. "It was fine after that, but it was not a good feeling to be there at that moment."

Ruth says there is also a female spirit who appears in the same room at the Pepper House. "I haven't a clue who the male presence is, but one of the children of Capt. Bang Pepper died at sea—a baby. And I think the female presence might be the wife looking for her child. That is just what I felt when I was there." Sea captain Bang Pepper built his Federal-style house in 1793. Because sea voyages often lasted several lonely years, ship captains were known to bring along their wives and children. Historical records indicate that a few unfortunate babies were born and died at sea.

With three properties to manage, guests to satisfy, and ghosts to appease, Ruth and her husband had little time to breathe. "As the restaurant at the Bramble Inn became so much busier, we would be doing eighty dinners a night, and then the two of us would get up early in the morning to serve thirty people for breakfast, and that was a complimentary breakfast—so when do you sleep? It was overwhelming over a few years." The solution to their harried

One of the lovely dining spaces at the inn.

existence was to sell the Pepper House and the 1849 House. "We wanted to concentrate all our efforts on the Bramble Inn and the restaurant."

In 2012, the prestigious Zagat guide voted the Bramble Inn the "Best Restaurant on Cape Cod," and in 2013, executive chef Ruth Manchester was inducted into Best Chefs America. "It's just such an honor to be nominated by other chefs. It's a profession that is not an easy one, long hours . . . but I love it when I am cooking all the time. My husband keeps saying, 'Sit and relax,' and I say, 'You know, I don't think I know how.' I just don't. It's hard for me to sit still. I have a high energy."

For Ruth, with fame came a loss: she misses her ghosts. "I haven't had any experiences in a number of years, and I am a little sad about that because I felt like they needed to communicate with me for some reason, and I was more than willing to let them."

Recently, one of the overnight guests at the Bramble Inn let Ruth know that she has a fairly powerful ghost lurking upstairs. The first floor of the inn is completely devoted to intimate dining spaces, the Bayside Bar, and the kitchen and prep areas. The second floor has three guest rooms: the Cabbage Rose Room, the Rooster Room, and the Washstand Room.

The disturbed guest, a football player on his honeymoon, was staying in the Cabbage Rose Room. "He came down after the first night and said he really felt a threatening presence." The innkeeper asked if he would like to check out, but the newlywed told her, "My wife didn't feel it. She is comfortable, so I'll try again."

There is admiration for the staying power of the groom in Ruth's voice as she relates the story of the jealous ghost. "For three nights, this poor guy was haunted by a presence who didn't want him anywhere near his new wife." Both Ruth and Cliff were sympathetic to the plight of the husband. "We couldn't wait for every morning when he would come down for breakfast, and we'd ask him, 'Did you see him again?' He'd say, 'Oh, yes. He was right there.'" The sleep-deprived football player could only describe his paranormal tormenter as "a presence, a heavy feeling," something or someone trying to get between him and his bride. Ruth attempts to suppress a chuckle. "I don't think it was a very good honeymoon, but he was very good-natured about it."

Neither of the Manchesters has ever been bothered by any negative energy or feelings when entering the Cabbage Rose Room, named for its Victorian floral wallpaper. Instead, what they have noticed is the smell. "There is a closet in the Cabbage Rose Room that we have repainted many times, but when you open that closet, it smells like pastry—Danish pastry, year-round. It is the funniest thing, even when we repaint it, it doesn't matter. It will smell like paint when we are doing it, but as soon as the paint dries, it goes back to the pastry smell. I have taken more people in that room and open the closet door, and I turn to them and say, 'Now, tell me what you smell?' and they always say it's like pastries baking." As the executive chef, Ruth Manchester creates many enticing entrees and appetizers, but Danish pastries are not included in her extensive repertoire of recipes. "It is just so strange." The chef ventures a guess. "I don't know—maybe whoever haunts that room was a baker."

Built in 1861 as a private residence for the Knowles family, the Bramble Inn became a meeting place for locals when Brewster's first telephone was installed. It operated as an inn and dining spot known as the 1861 House, offering meals and lodging to travelers year-round. In the mid-1970s, Karen Etsell and Elaine Brennan reconfigured it as the Bramble Inn Gallery and Café, open only in the summer months. When the Manchesters purchased it in 1985, they reopened it as a year-round inn and full-service restaurant. Neither the previous owners nor its present owners are aware of any baker on the premises, especially one who had a fondness for whipping up Danish pastries. So the identity of the mysterious baker and his ghostly concoctions is left unresolved. At least, says Ruth, "It is a lovely smell. Who doesn't love a warm Danish pastry?"

Ruth Manchester has a great attitude when it comes to the ghosts that have followed her around. "We've had an interesting life with that aspect of what is going on." As for their future plans for the Bramble Inn and Restaurant, she is philosophical. "We decided we really love what we are doing, and we'll just keep doing it until we

The closet in the Cabbage Rose Room has an aroma of Danish pastries.

can't do it anymore. I'll be the ghost haunting it. I am sure I will be. They will take me out of here feet first, but I'll be back in spirit form and torture the new owners." Ruth rethinks what she has just said. "No, I'll be a good ghost. I'll just be pointing out what they need to take care of."

Lagniappe: The Manchesters were familiar with the Bramble Gallery and Café prior to purchasing it. "Cliff and I were running the dining room at the Old Manse Inn down the road, which was owned by his parents, and so every now and then we'd go into the Bramble for lunch, so we became friendly with the owners, Karen and Elaine. We reconnected with Elaine because she had gone to school with my brother." Over lunch, Ruth and Cliff indulged in a little wishful thinking. "We always used to say to them, 'Oh, you know, we love to be at the Old Manse with Cliff's parents, but we'd really love to have our own place someday.' Elaine looked at me, and she said, 'You will. You'll have it someday.'" When the Bramble went on the market in 1984, the Manchesters made an offer, although they did have a few questions about the building's status. "We asked them if the place was haunted, and they said no; they had always been comfortable." Apparently, Karen and Elaine had had no encounters with the beleaguered honeymooner's tormentor or with the baker and his delicious aromas. Ghosts or no ghosts, Cliff and Ruth were ready. "Of course, we already managed dinner service at the Old Manse. We had a loyal following, so they just followed us half a mile down the road. It worked out very well."

The Ocean Edge Resort and Golf Club in Brewster.

15

Addie on Patrol

A female spirit reputedly hovers over the manicured grounds of the Ocean Edge Resort and Golf Club in Brewster. A devastating fire in 1906 left her home in ruins. Now, Addie Nickerson is on patrol to ensure that it never happens again.

The 1866 nuptials of Addie Daniels and Roland Nickerson began with a mandolin processional at the Daniels' home in Brewster. Coverage of the formal afternoon affair by a *New York Telegraph* correspondent elicited an adverse reaction in a number of households with eligible daughters. The scathing tone of the lead sentence was not flattering: "For the last five years Mr. Nickerson has been considered one of the choice fish in the social swim, and all sorts of bait have been thrown at him."

This same reporter went on to comment that the groom "lived in a marble palace" and "never had to learn the lesson of privation." The lavish wedding gifts added to the writer's ire. Perhaps, given his meager salary, having to list "a hunk of bank stock" amid the many presents received by the privileged couple proved too much for sincere civility. Among the jewels showered on the bride were a pearl necklace with a diamond clasp, a token from the groom; diamond solitaire earrings from her father-in-law; and a lace pin of flowers with diamond hearts from her mother-in-law. The ultimate gift was yet to come.

Roland C. Nickerson was the son of one of Chicago's most prominent and wealthy couples: Samuel Mayo Nickerson and Matilda Crosby Nickerson. As the president and co-founder of the First National Bank of Chicago, Samuel could afford to indulge his only child. According to Nickerson family lore, Samuel was fond of vacationing on Cape Cod. One morning, in the late 1880s Samuel stood on a bluff in Brewster overlooking Cape Cod Bay. He stuck his gold-tipped cane into the ground and declared that a house should be built there for Roland; his wife, Addie; and their three children, Roland Jr., Samuel, and Helen.

Completed in 1890, Fieldstone Hall, despite its name, was actually a wooden Victorian mansion. It boasted three floors, four chimneys, a wide verandah, covered porches, and a balcony over the front entrance. Photos from the Nickerson family album also show a carriage house with an attached stone tower from which they enjoyed the coastal view. In addition, the forty-eight-acre parcel featured a pond, a private beach, and a nine-hole golf course. Upkeep of the enormous home and grounds required a staff of twenty-two servants.

Roland and Addie entertained often and on a scale unsurpassed anywhere on the Cape. A bugler would raise a brass horn to his lips to announce the arrival of each carriage at the ornate iron gates. Coachmen dressed in tails and top hats would escort the guests. Specially chartered trains often brought visitors from all over the country to the Nickersons' summer retreat. Grover Cleveland, in between his two non-consecutive terms as president, was among the honored luminaires.

On May 10, 1906, Roland and Addie's world collapsed. Fieldstone Hall burned to the ground, leaving only the foundation intact. The fire started in a kindling pile in the southwest corner and then snaked its way into the cellar near a huge stack of coal. The conflagration quickly consumed the wooden structure.

In an interview many years after the fire, local resident Ray Crown recalled that he was down on the beach collecting oysters when "The flames leapt and the smoke billowed. Mr. Roland Nickerson just sat on the lawn and watched it burn down." Along with the house, the fire claimed the family's clothing, rare old china, and a myriad of paintings and books. The financial lost topped out at $500,000, only $3,000 of which was covered by the Nickersons' insurance policy. The Brewster newspaper reported that as the house was ". . . licked up by flames, Hon. Roland C. Nickerson, sick from heart disease, waved farewell and circled around the scene in his automobile to safety."

Roland, Addie, the children, and the servants all survived, but Roland, already ill and weak, seemed unable to bear the loss. Two weeks later, he was dead. His obituary stated that "Mr. Nickerson's illness . . . was aggravated by the shock of the fire . . . and his death followed yesterday." Under such tragic circumstances, it would seem that the ghost hovering over the grounds would be Roland's distraught spirit seeking a way to save his home, but the only reported ghost sightings are that of his widow, Addie.

Unlike her husband, Addie remained undaunted by the devastation. With the assistance of her father-in-law, Samuel Nickerson, she immediately set about designing a new residence to be built on top of the footprint of the original Fieldstone Hall. With the fire etched indelibly in their minds, the pair took extraordinary precautions to prevent future risks. The new structure was built with reinforced steel and concrete and had walls four feet thick, covered by a stucco façade. By 1907 standards, this was as fireproof as anything could be, and it was measurably larger. The second Fieldstone Hall had sixteen rooms and seven bedrooms, all sumptuously outfitted with marble fireplaces, individual bathrooms, and walk-in closets. Italian artisans were brought in to carve the intricate oak woodwork for the massive staircase, ceilings, and interior trim.

The first floor contained a hunting room for trophies with the Nickerson family crest on the hooded fireplace mantel, formal dining room, breakfast room, ladies parlor, library, billiard room, and two-story main reception area. One account says that the billiard room was so large that it was used by the Nickerson children and their friends as a roller-skating arena. The immense carriage house next door had survived the fire, but it was given a face lift to complement the elaborate Tudor style of the new mansion.

Addie's mother-in-law, Matilda Crosby Nickerson, passed away just as the revived Fieldstone Hall was completed in 1912. Her father-in-law, Samuel, lived just two years after that. For Addie, the

The ghost of Addie Daniels Nickerson patrols the grounds.

The hunting room, where Addie and Roland displayed their trophies.

The Nickerson family crest.

loss of Samuel meant losing her staunchest supporter. Together, they had envisioned and directed the construction of a palatial new home that could withstand the threat of any fire. Addie resided at Fieldstone Hall until shortly before her death in 1938. Then, rumors of Addie's ghost patrolling Fieldstone Hall began.

The estate remained in the Nickerson family until Roland Nickerson's granddaughter sold it to the La Salette missionaries in 1945. In austere contrast to the heyday of the mansion's elaborate party days, young seminarians prayed, studied, and worked in the house and around the gardens. The missionaries may have inadvertently contributed to the alleged haunting of Fieldstone Hall: the La Salette religious order was founded to honor a mysterious apparition believed to be the Virgin Mary. The figure of a lady appeared before two peasant children at La Salette, near Grenoble, France, on September 19, 1846. When the La Salettes established a novitiate at Fieldstone Hall, they brought their tradition of honoring the apparition with them.

In 1980, Corcoran Jennison purchased the property, and in 1986, he established the Ocean Edge Resort and Golf Club. The refurbished Fieldstone Hall served as the centerpiece of a modern-day recreation complex. With the hall once again resounding with the laughter and voices of guests, interest in the original hostess, Addie Daniels Nickerson, increased.

The resort manager, hoping to capitalize on Addie's story, came out with a novel way to promote the hotel and increase business in the off-season: a "Spooky Mansion" package.

The Ocean Edge Resort and Club dares ghost hunters to visit its haunted mansion to try and catch a glimpse of the resident ghost, Addie. The Spooky Mansion package boasts deluxe accommodations, daily breakfast for two, a jack-o-lantern of treats and complimentary late-night coffee, and flashlights for night owls on the lookout for Addie. Those who show 'proof' of spotting the capricious haunter will enjoy their entire stay on the house . . . the haunted house that is. Ouija boards are available at the front desk for guests who want to have a séance to reach out to Addie.

Travel Magazine picked up on the promotional piece and ran it under the headline: "Stay Is on the House for Spirit Seekers Who Spot Addie the Ghost." Bryan Webb, the resort's current Director of Sales and Marketing, admits that the story will not die. "People want to claim that Addie Nickerson haunts the mansion as well as the Carriage House. Yes, it is a one-hundred-year-old building, and we've all had our brushes with Addie, but we no longer go out there and say the house is haunted because it is not." Webb is adamant that this is against the current policy of the resort. "Haunted Weekends? We don't do that."

Webb clearly wishes the "Spooky Mansion" marketing ploy never happened. "Many, many years ago they had haunted weekends here under previous management. Under this management, we don't promote it. We complete disassociate ourselves with that because no one actually physically sleeps in Fieldstone Hall anymore. There are no guest rooms in this building." Webb is referring to the current status of the historic home as a banquet, dining, and conference facility. Guests check-in by the main lobby, then leave to go to one of the 337 guest rooms located in the Mansion Wing adjacent to the hall or to separate villas around the grounds.

Webb is protective when it comes to people chasing Addie around as if she is some kind of prize. "Poor little Addie. She's got a bad rep around here. You hear people say she turns the lights on and off." One visiting medium claimed that Addie was responsible for a falling chandelier and for making the elevator doors in the carriage house flash open with no one pushing the buttons. Webb does not buy into any of it.

"Those ghost hunter groups," says Webb, "contact me regularly." The marketing director's standard response is very diplomatic. "We tell them there is nothing to investigate." Webb insists that they rarely get guests asking if Addie's ghost is still around. "I've been here [since 2007], and I've only had one guy send me an email that he had an 'experience' here."

Webb places the emphasis on the amenities. "We are a four-diamond full-service resort. We have just completed a $55 million

Addie's ghost allegedly plays tricks inside the carriage house.

renovation. We have six pools, tennis courts, a complete golf facility, conference space, and a private beach on Cape Cod Bay." At the same time, looking over the many Nickerson family portraits and photos on display, the marketing director says, "We kind of attach ourselves to the history of the Nickersons."

Samuel and Matilda's portraits hang opposite each other on the landing of the grand staircase in the lobby. Informal family photos of the Nickersons at play on the beach, riding bikes, sailing, and dining alfresco on the terrace are showcased on tables and tucked on shelves in the formal library, now an intimate dining room. The most touching image is of a bemused Addie, sitting in a rocking chair on the terrace. Taken shortly before her death, she appears to be contemplating the marvel of her home and its rise, literally, from the ashes. Nickerson descendants gave the photos to the resort. Webb says, "They wanted people who stayed here now to see how their family enjoyed their time here."

Webb agrees that Samuel and Addie would be well pleased, but, he reluctantly adds, "Roland, probably not. He drank himself to death after the fire. If there was an unhappy ghost on the property, it would have to be Roland."

As to whether Addie's spirit darts about the hall and grounds, double-checking that the guests are safe and that no little spark of fire lurks in the corners, Webb restates the official position of the resort: "When the previous manager had the 'Spooky Mansion' package, it was just a marketing ploy, a good way to get people in during Halloween. I've never had a run-in with a ghost here, and very few people that have worked here can claim that, either."

Webb has an interesting rationale for why there is so much interest in Cape Cod ghosts. "A lot of times, you get into fads. Lately, there's a fad in hotels with ice bars. The Hilton has one. You go into a special room that is thirty degrees. You pay an extra fee to go in. You rent a fur coat. Ice bars will run their course. Ghosts will run their course."

The grand staircase in Fieldstone Hall.

Lagniappe: In addition to the legacy of Fieldstone Hall, Addie and Roland Nickerson were the largest private owners of forest land on the Cape in the early twentieth century. In 1934, Addie and her daughter, Helen, donated more than seventeen hundred acres to the Commonwealth of Massachusetts. Addie wanted to honor the memory of her son, who died in the 1918 flu epidemic. Today, the Nickerson State Park functions as a multi-use conservation, camping, and hiking area. When Addie and Roland purchased the land, they created a private hunting, trapping, and fishing preserve for themselves and invited guests. Addie was a "crack shot" and an avid sportswoman who often led the way for the day's adventure. Some believe that the spirit of the woman with "a backbone of steel" continues to roam freely through the woods, as well as keeping tabs on her beloved Fieldstone Hall.

16

A Trio of Ghosts at the Orleans Inn

Despite its volatile past— murder, multiple suicides, and troublesome ghosts—the Orleans Waterfront Inn is a happy place. Built in 1875 by a sea captain whose lineage reaches back to *Mayflower* passenger Constance Hopkins Snow, this converted mansion overlooks serene Nauset Harbor and the Orleans Town Cove. When one of the inn's resident spirits ventures out to mix and mingle with inn guests, current owner Ed Maas is cordial. Now, he is on a first-name basis with all three entities: Fred, Paul, and Hannah.

The Orleans Waterfront Inn has a trio of resident ghosts.

Full disclosure of the inn's haunted status wasn't forthcoming until after Maas had placed a deposit with the bank to purchase the foreclosed structure in the summer of 1996. Instead of congratulations on his great deal, Ed and his family were greeted by locals with puzzled wonder: "Are you crazy? The place is haunted!"

Maas questioned his realtor, who conceded that "There were rumors." Amazed by his realtor's casual attitude, Maas retorted, "There are full page articles in the *Cape Cod Times!*" The realtor dismissed his concerns. "Oh, I seem to have heard some things. Nothing to worry about." Feeling that they were left with few options, the Maas family forged ahead. The parents and older children gathered with flashlights to conduct their own impromptu paranormal investigation. No spooky apparitions popped out to scare them away.

A few weeks later, Ed's wife, Laurie, returned with a friend for a walk-through of the property. As they approached the third floor, a frigid blast of air shot through the hallway leading to the guest rooms. Laurie, who Ed describes as a "conservative New England Protestant," offered a surprising rationalization: it was a ghost seeking the warmth of their bodies. Although previously a reluctant partner in the renovation venture, Laurie became fully committed to rescuing the inn so that their "ghost would always have a home."

"We didn't know who she was then, so I named her Hannah," explains Ed. "I saw the name Hannah on a Snow family headstone, and I liked it. She's not a Snow, but we use the name." Hannah proceeded to whip out a few more tricks to get their attention. "She likes the candles lit. The wait staff will blow out the candles on the tables at the end of service in the Snow dining room then turn around and all the flames will be relit. Occasionally, they have to blow them out two or three times before she stops."

Hannah's other paranormal preferences have been a bit more problematic. "In the 1990s, this place was in terrible shape—an embarrassment to the community. There had been so many owners. One of them even painted the cupola purple!" One of the first things Maas did was to buy all new locks for the doors to secure the building. Uneasy about his recent investment and unable to sleep,

Ed Maas named the female ghost Hannah after seeing this headstone.

Maas returned in the evening to see every door wide open. "The power hadn't been turned on yet, so I got my flashlight and went inside. I heard footsteps and voices upstairs. Of course, I was thinking someone broke in. I had my hand on the phone ready to call the police." For reasons with which he still struggles, Maas had a change of heart. He no longer believed that the break-in had a human connection. "It was Hannah, maybe, entertaining her guests." This new owner relinquished control for the remainder of the early morning hours to his lively female spirit. "I went across the street to the Stop and Shop." Maas watched and waited until daylight to return to the inn. He never saw anyone exit the building.

The Maas family believes that their female apparition was a "lady of the evening" in her former life. "What happened was that, in the 1920s, the inn was a house of ill repute. Wives would tell their husbands, 'Don't you go over there, that's a house full of sin.'" Maas attempts to mask a smile. "And it was—it was a brothel." The Irish Mafia allegedly operated behind the scenes, while the police looked the other way. One of the "ladies" of the house was murdered by a disgruntled customer. The case never went to court. Perhaps because her murderer was never punished, Hannah's spirit has been unable to move on. Maas is grateful. "It is because of Hannah that the inn is here today; she made her presence known to Laurie, and Laurie decided we had to save the inn so Hannah had a place to stay." Laurie even issued an order to her husband: "Don't piss off the ghost." Maas chuckles when he repeats this commandment. "I always listen to my wife."

On May 15, 1997, the inn's pub, the Tavern on the Cove, and the Snow Dining Room were the first spaces to reopen with the Maas family at the helm. In the weeks that followed, customers poured in. Snippets of conversation hung in the recharged atmosphere. Locals seated at the bar and grouped around the tables agreed that there had always been something about the inn that was "magical and mystical." They may have been reminiscing about the inn's glory days in the 1950s, when Hollywood's elite, including Elizabeth Taylor, Montgomery Clift, and Frank Sinatra's parents, were said to be frequent guests. Or, they may have been alluding to the inn's uncanny ability to reinvent itself, to rise from the real threat of demolition and regain its status in the community. The returning customers did stop short of saying that the inn's salvation might be divine intervention or paranormal possession. After all, it is New England, and speculation that a mere building could be more than timber and nails and provide a breeding ground for ghosts—well, such thoughts are best left unsaid.

Once Ed Maas got past the daunting financial challenge of restoring a multi-level inn and restaurant, he was intrigued by the history of the six-story home. In 1875, Capt. Aaron Snow celebrated the completion of his Victorian mansion, capped by a two-story belvedere. A few skeptics called it "Aaron's Folly," but it remains the tallest structure in the area. The main floor became the general store for the town. On the upper floors, Aaron lived with his beloved wife, Mary, and raised their seven children. In 1892, the devoted couple died within weeks of each other, Aaron on May 10, and Mary, June 1.

Locals discussed the ghosts while sitting at this bar.

Maas's most meaningful discovery was that Aaron Snow, the builder of the house, was a direct descendant of Constance Hopkins Snow, who arrived in Provincetown in 1620 aboard the *Mayflower* at age fourteen. Her stepbrother, Oceanus, was the first baby born on the *Mayflower*. Constance's future husband, Nicholas Snow, arrived on the *Ann* in 1623. The young couple married in 1627 and then moved to the Nauset area, now known as Orleans. The Snows were one of seven families to establish deep roots on the Cape. In 1966, Snow family descendants placed a marker for Constance Snow in the Old Cove Burying Ground near the Orleans Inn. Maas learned about it from a guest. "Virginia Snow stayed here. She told me where Constance was buried, and whenever I pass by the old burying ground, I stop by and visit for a while. I feel close to Constance and the other Pilgrims buried there."

Maas had already located Aaron's gravesite in the Snow family plot in the Orleans cemetery. Standing by the obelisk for the first

Constance Snow's grave marker in the Old Cove Burying Ground.

time, Maas felt compelled to talk to Aaron and to reassure him that he was taking care of his home. "We'll do our best." After several guests remarked that Ed Maas (who is not a Snow descendant) bore a strong resemblance to the portrait of patriarch Aaron, an eerie realization crept over Maas—he was the same age when he bought the Orleans Inn as Aaron Snow was when he built it in 1875. For Maas, the gap between the centuries closed; past and present merged.

Captain Snow built his home high so that his wife, Mary, could watch his sailing vessel, the *Nettie M. Rogers,* safely navigate the treacherous Nauset shoals on its return voyage. "The family would see the ship and place a tree up in the window of the belvedere as a welcome home signal. They were happy to have him back." Maas cannot fathom how anyone could repeatedly carry a tree—even a small one—up the impossibly narrow flight of stairs to the cupola, so he improvised. "I wanted to let Aaron Snow know that he would always be welcome at the Orleans Inn. I bought one of those put-together artificial Christmas trees, carried it up piece by piece, and assembled it in front of the window."

For the curious visitor, fair warning: if you choose to navigate the steep and less-than-shoulder-width stairs to the belvedere, duck when you reach the top. The opening is small, and if you miscalculate, the jarring encounter of head and overhead beam hurts. The reward for your pain is the sight of a fully-decorated Christmas tree, a panoramic view of the cove, and a deep sense that Aaron's cherished wife, Mary, and their children have been there many times before you.

However, while the belvedere served as the site of many joyous homecoming celebrations, not all experiences there were positive ones. In the 1950s, Fred, the bartender of the restaurant downstairs, tied a rope around the thick, exposed, wooden beam and hung himself. His distraught spirit remains.

"We have guests who say they talk to Fred up there, but the only real proof we have is when the *Ghost Hunters* team from the SyFy channel stayed here for two weeks. The episode they filmed is called 'The Inn of the Dead.' They asked Fred a question, and he answered." Maas pauses. He gazes out the window of the Snow

Mary Snow's view from a window in the top floor of the belvedere.

The impossibly steep staircase leads to the top floor of the belvedere.

Fred, a former bartender, hung himself in the belvedere. His ghost lingers there.

Dining Room to the boats bobbing at their moorings buoys in the waters of the cove. His eyes drift up to the belvedere several floors overhead. "They had a recording of Fred and they played it back for me. It sounded like he was saying, 'Get me down. Get me down.'"

Fred also occasionally returns to his bartending duties. Megan, one of Maas's twin daughters, along with a few patrons, have witnessed glasses sliding across the bar as if being pushed, but no human hand has been within reach. Maas points out that the *Ghost Hunters* investigative team tried to replicate the glasses moving by themselves. They said it might just be condensation on the bar top and the glasses sliding in it." Maas shakes his head. "I don't know about that—something was going on, and Megan saw it." Visitors with a penchant for the paranormal are invited to climb into the belvedere and report back if they see Fred "hanging out" or lingering in the bar near closing.

Sadly, Fred's suicide was followed by that of Paul, who worked as a dishwasher in the restaurant. Paul also chose hanging as a means to a tragic end. His ghostly alter ego appears as a shadow in the basement, the site of his final moments. Two of the investigators confirmed that they saw a dark shadow pass back and forth in front of the basement window. The kitchen staff believes that it is Paul's ghost who arbitrarily slams the door if it has been left open for too long.

The Orleans Waterfront Inn has seen many reincarnations under a diverse range of owners. After the deaths of their parents, none of Aaron and Mary Snow's children could live there without them. For eight years, the house sat forlorn and unoccupied. In 1900, two elderly sisters—Maas refers to them as Clara and Emma—purchased the Snow mansion and ran it as a boarding house, where they lived in genteel splendor along with their many cats.

"We found out about that the first New Year's Eve we were open. A gentleman came in and told us about them." The customer neglected to mention anything about lingering feline spirits, but Maas soon learned that paranormal activities can extend to pets. "When we were redoing one of the bathrooms, the workmen kept saying they heard cats crying. One of them even said he saw a shadow in the shape of a cat. I told them 'No, we don't have any cats on the property.'" A frustrated Maas says it went on during the entire renovation process. The workmen kept prodding him, "Sure you don't have any cats?" If the crying emanated from one of Clara or Emma's cats, they had far surpassed their limit of nine lives.

During Prohibition, the sedate boarding house had new owners with livelier pursuits. Wild parties and booze prevailed. Bootleg whiskey flowed. When Federal agents arrived on the scene, a secret space in the lobby concealed the contraband liquor. The reputation of this once-private residence, the pride of Aaron Snow, seemed forever tarnished.

Shortly after World War II, Bruno Burkhart saw the potential in the disreputable establishment. Although there were some in the community who did not embrace a German as the new owner, strong-willed Bruno and his wife, Ella, dug in. They renovated the existing rooms and added two wings to the mansion. The final result was a twenty-two-thousand-square-foot luxury hotel. Ed Maas approves. "They knew what they were doing." However, with changing economic times, a revolving door of owners—some lasting just a few months—once again led to a precarious situation and eventual foreclosure.

The Maas family has restored the inn to its Victorian grandeur. The Tavern on the Cove, the Snow Dining Room, and the covered deck with its magnificent view of the cove have all earned rave reviews. The upper levels of the inn have remained essentially untouched (minus a few redecorating and refurbishing details) from the original 1875 construction. Maas confirms that they made no structural changes to the guest rooms except for room number six, which had been two smaller rooms. They removed the dividing wall—and lost a ghost. According to prevailing rumors, the small rooms were haunted. Maas was told that if one makes a structural change, the ghost or troubled entity is disturbed and leaves. This is not the case with rooms four and five. Guests continue to relate tales of ghostly activity during their stay. "Either of these rooms could have been Hannah's room," states Maas. "We just don't know."

The Cove Inn, the Ellis Inn, the Orleans Inn of the Yankee Fisherman, the Orleans Waterfront Inn—neither the signage outside nor the parade of owners has had any effect on the undisturbed spirits within. Fred, Paul, and Hannah have settled in for the long haul.

Hannah continues to test the boundaries of just what Laurie and Ed Maas will tolerate. When the inn is at full capacity, Ed will occasionally camp out on the sofa in the lobby with one eye judiciously focused on the front door in the event that Hannah's twitchy fingers gravitate to the bolt locks and throw them open.

One night in particular stands out. A naked female guest strolled into the dining room. As she passed, the diplomatic owner greeted her. "I said, 'Hello,' and she said, 'Hello.'" At the time, Maas believed the encounter was just "another perk of being an innkeeper." Several weeks passed, and a staff member informed him that they might have a bigger problem. A family stopped by the front of the inn and looked up to see a naked woman dancing in the belvedere. "You need to put some curtains up there." Maas is now convinced that the "naked lady" episodes were none other than their very own Hannah, upping the ante on her paranormal performances.

Lagniappe: The Orleans Waterfront Inn has eleven guest suites on the third floor and a five-room family suite on the Mansard Level, directly below the belvedere. No guarantees are given as to whether any of the rooms come with a ghost. "Activity happens when you least expect it," says Maas. "A lot of times, we don't even notice anymore." For the truly curious, the secret storage space for the Prohibition-era bootleg contraband is to your left as you enter the lobby. The picture frame wainscoting with wallpaper inserts conceals the entrance. The space has been repurposed as the inn's coat room. Before you leave, make sure to ask about the painting of the dancing ghosts, Fred, Paul, and Hannah!

Capt. Ebenezer Harding Linnell.

17

Love Possessed

There are ghosts and there is love,
And both are present here.
To those who listen, this tale will tell
The truth of love and if it's near.
—Nicholas Sparks, *A Bend in the Road*

"Love like ours can never die!" Impaled by a spoke from his own ship's wheel, Capt. Ebenezer Linnell might have shouted this lover's litany to his beloved in his final fatal moments. His adoring wife, Rebecca, kept him close to her heart, never faltering in her devotion. Her ghostly form waits for him at the Captain Linnell House in East Orleans.

Ebenezer Harding Linnell, born in 1811 on Barley Neck Road, Orleans, married the beautiful, golden-haired Rebecca Crosby in 1835. She was twenty-one, and he was twenty-four, a young sea captain embarking on a promising career. The couple moved into a Cape Codder on the site of the present day Captain Linnell House. For the next two decades, Eben would sail around the globe on the clipper ships *Flying Mist* and *Eagle Wing*. At first, petite, four-foot-eleven-inch Rebecca accompanied her husband, but as their children grew—Helen, Florentina, Ebenezer, and Abigail—Rebecca was content to remain at home. Eben and Rebecca's love letters, preserved in Boston's Peabody Museum, are a testament to the couple's enduring devotion. Eben sought only the best for the love of his life.

Rebecca Crosby Linnell.

On a trip to France in 1850, he stayed at a shipping agent's villa in the port city of Marseilles. Captain Linnell brought the house plans back to the Cape and had his father-in-law oversee the construction of a neo-classical French villa. "They built around the Cape Codder. It's still here." Shelly Conway along with her husband, Bill, own the Captain Linnell House, now an award-winning restaurant. "Actually," says a thoughtful Shelly, "Captain Linnell was considered a show-off. Everyone in town thought he was too grand for his britches. He filled the house with furniture and fittings from Europe and the Orient." A cupola on the roof of the villa allowed Rebecca to look out over their thirty-five acres of land and beyond to the shores of Cape Cod Bay near the present Skaket Beach. "Rebecca would sit up there, and when her husband's ship would come in, she would be able to see because at that time there were no trees around here. There was a 360-degree view."

The Captain Linnell House, now an award-winning restaurant.

In 1864, in one of the ceaseless ironies of the sea, Captain Linnell announced to his family that he was embarking on his last voyage. Off the coast of Brazil, a tropical storm tossed the ship about like a toy. The boom holding the spanker sail broke loose and smashed the captain against his wheel, where a spoke punctured one his lungs. Ebeneezer Linnell was critically injured and lived only a few days. The fifty-three-year-old master mariner was buried at sea. According to an article published in the December 1995 edition of the *Linnell Family Newsletter*, Rebecca retreated to the cupola to "read and reread the letter from the *Eagle Wing*'s first mate." The letter described Captain Linnell's "horrible and untimely death."

Restaurateur Shelly Conway describes how "after he died, Rebecca would go up to the cupola every single day for the rest of her life." Rebecca Cosby Linnell died at the age of eighty-one. The *Linnell Family Newsletter* also reports that Rebecca's lonely spirit still visits the widow's walk "wistfully looking out to sea." She searches the horizon for her captain, who will never return. Wishful visitors, however, have a problem—the entrance to Rebecca's observation post is blocked. "There is a wonderful inside staircase that leads to the cupola," explains Conway, "but the last private owners, the Hamiltons, actually put a chimney up through there." Viewed from the outside, the chimney stack is clearly visible poking through the cupola's roof. The physical obstruction has had little impact on Rebecca's spirit, as people have claimed to see Rebecca seated in the cupola, staring out to sea.

Bill and Shelly Conway purchased the captain's mansion in June 1988. "It was derelict, basically on its last legs. It had been a restaurant for over fifty years, and it was supposed to be turnkey, but it wasn't." Shelly recalls that even its name was a misunderstanding. "Our realtor told us he was taking us to see the Captain's alehouse. As soon as we heard that, we said, 'We are not interested in an alehouse.' The real estate agent got flustered, and said, 'No, no, no. It's not the *ale*house, it's the *Linnell* house, and it's a fine dining restaurant.' My husband, Bill, is a master chef, and I am a restoration gardener, so we were happy we weren't going to see a tavern, but

The cupola where Rebecca's ghost maintains her vigil.

still the place was a disappointment. It was so overgrown it looked haunted."

When asked if she was aware of any stories about the mansion, Shelly jumps right in. "Ghosts? When we first came here there truly was a ghost. There was a sense of coldness when you walked from room to room. We lived upstairs over the restaurant with our four kids. My youngest had just turned four, so I would walk around here at all hours of the night. There would be a sense that somebody had just left the room. You would see a door close, a curtain flutter as if someone passed by. It wasn't frightening—it was more like sadness."

Shelly sighs as her eyes are drawn to the logs crackling in the huge fireplace in the ballroom. She turns back with a smile. "As we fixed it up, the sadness got less and less. We had been here

The stairs lead to the Conways' private quarters.

about ten years, and I was up about two-thirty in the morning, and I can remember realizing the coldness was gone. There was more of a sense of warmth, like total acceptance, appreciative that we had loved and cared for this house again." Shelly feels that the house is now as romantic for her and her husband as it was for its original owners.

The Conways have created an enchanting ambiance, hosting intimate dinners, elegant parties, and treasured weddings. They also have reestablished a lovely custom. Based on some of Rebecca's letters, Shelly learned that it was the captain's habit to send his bride roses. "We always have pink roses. That's our trademark because it's the particular flower Rebecca loved." The Conways order upwards of five dozen roses a week and collect all of the petals because "people like to throw them at the weddings."

At one blissful affair, there were more than scattered petals left behind. "After that particular wedding, a guest insisted he saw

Rebecca's favorite flowers in the dining room.

someone dressed like a bride on the lawn." This would have been a natural sight, says an agreeable Shelly, but "the bride had already left." Attempts were made to mollify the guest. "It was like, okay, okay, and then we sort of questioned him about maybe he had been drinking a little, but he seemed totally sane and rational, except even after we explained that the bride and groom had driven off, he wouldn't let it go. He kept saying, "I just saw her on the front lawn." Shelly believes that he saw a figure in a long, white gown and assumed it was the bride. Could the stunning apparition have been Rebecca drawn to the fragrant roses? For Shelly, that would be a lovely bonus. After all, readers of *Cape Cod Life* have voted the Captain Linnell House as the most romantic wedding venue on the Cape.

In addition to the mysterious bride, other diners have reported looking out the windows and seeing people coming up the path from the beach. Again, this is a perfectly ordinary occurrence—with one small caveat. Shelly says that her guests would describe the approaching men as wearing clothing similar to the impeccable style of Captain Linnell. The *Linnell Family Newsletter* also alludes to tales about the captain's ghost "walking the grounds and rooms of the Linnell mansion."

Shelly and Bill Conway fell in love with a sea captain's mansion and bought the once-neglected home on a "young and crazy whim." It appears that it needed them as much as they needed it. Amid the fragrant, sweet smells of trailing wisteria, lavender, and roses, the Captain Linnell House of today nourishes the heart. Eben and Rebecca are reunited; their portraits hang side by side in the inviting lobby of this premier Cape Cod restaurant. "This is a happy place to work. And, to continue making people feel good and giving them a place to create special moments is an honor."

Lagniappe: Capt. Eben Linnell was reputed to be unequaled among American ship masters for native ability, energy, and shrewdness. In 1855, he raced his most famous clipper ship, the Massachusetts-built *Eagle Wing,* from London to Hong Kong in 83½ days, a record that

Rebecca and Eben, reunited at the Captain Linnell House.

still stands. While at home in a rare lull between voyages, he invented an improved top-sail rig, which was patented and incorporated in the design of sixty-four ships. A scale model of the *Eagle Wing* is on display in the enclosed garden dining room, a former terrace. The Conways are delighted to have been able to preserve a part of Cape Cod history. Chef Bill Conway oversees the kitchen, turning out classic American cuisine, and Shelly oversees the front of house and the lush gardens. Shelly holds a picture of the house as it looked in 1852. "Where we are sitting in the ballroom was the barn. The passageway between our ballroom and the lobby was a carriage house and shed. If you are standing in the lobby, you are actually standing in the original Cape Codder. All the way to the left is the French villa addition, now our fine dining spaces." Shelly feels that it must have been particularly hard for Rebecca to finish the villa by herself, as her husband died before it was completed. This may account for the sadness Shelly sensed when she and her family first moved into the captain's house. Perhaps it stemmed from a previous owner, who died after a long addiction to alcohol. Shelly and Bill conclude their recap of the house's history on a lighter note. "I think something that stands out in my mind was when Matt Damon came here for his college roommate's wedding. All he did was stand out back and talk to the kitchen help, and for the last dance, he danced with his roommate's grandmother. He was a really great guy," says Bill. Shelly is next. "One of the restaurant owners before us would go down to the beach and dress up like Lady Godiva. So, we have had some colorful characters pass through here."

18

The House on the Hill in Eastham

"I came to see the ghost." Michael, nine years old, dressed in a red Patriots sweatshirt and faded jeans, is on a mission. Standing in the doorway of the Edward Penniman House in Eastham, his head pivots rapidly to the right and left, up and down. Michael's mother apologizes to the tour guide on duty. "He found an old copy of the book *The Ghost at the Penniman House* at my sister's house in Wellfleet, and he begged me to bring him here." The male volunteer stares blankly back

The haunted façade of the Penniman House in Eastham.

at the woman and her son. Michael's mother tries again. "It's a children's book about a little girl who sees a ghost digging in the garden at Penniman House." The elderly guide scratches at his neck and squints at Michael, who is shifting from one foot to the other, impatient to get inside. "Don't know about any ghost, but come on in."

Michael and his parents peer into the dimly lit space of the roped-off parlor, displaying its original Penniman-family furniture. The inquisitive boy is disappointed that he can't step inside and explore. The guide quickly assures him that he is free to roam the rest of the house, and Michael bounds up the stairs. He stomps back down a few minutes later, announcing that there is nothing up there.

Michael is partially correct. This former whaling captain's home is sparsely furnished. The majority of the artifacts were sold at auction prior to its acquisition by the National Park Service in 1963. The last occupant was Irma Broun, the granddaughter of Capt. Edward Penniman, who built the mansion in 1868. Because the park lacked the funds to properly seal the environment, it has been swept clean of most of the personal touches. Visiting hours are

Capt. Edward Penniman, seated in the parlor. (Photograph courtesy National Park Service)

limited to one afternoon a week. The house, with its washed-out red mansard roof, sits like a lonely old spinster sequestered from the rest of humanity. Its very isolation fuels its haunted reputation. A repeat visitor from Maryland concurs: "I've been to the old whaling captain's home and always get a strange feeling of sadness and a sense of being watched."

If the visitor was referring to the ghost of Captain Penniman, he likely would have found a very imposing apparition. E. G. Perry, in his 1898 book *A Trip Around Cape Cod,* described Penniman as "that arctic whaleman . . . a man whose record Cape Cod history will not let die." The captain's obituary read: "With his stalwart physique and commanding features, he looked every inch the sea captain of romance in the days of Cape Cod's prominence on the seas."

The damp sea air trails through the house and carries with it a foreboding chill. Visitors glance warily over their shoulders. In the late summer of 2013, in the final days before the home is boarded up for the long winter season ahead, a young couple from Connecticut hurries through the rooms. Their final stop is the parlor. "It feels like he's following us, as if he wants to make sure we don't touch any of his things." The husband towers over his wife and tells her that she is being paranoid. The young woman tugs at the bottom of her navy blue sweater and wraps the loose ends more tightly around her waist. "Seriously, did you look at the captain's picture? Those eyes—those are ghost eyes. This place is haunted. And it's not a friendly ghost, so it can't be his daughter, Bessie, even if she did die in the house. You heard the guide. He said she loved living here, so it's not her following us around. It's the captain. He wants the place to himself."

Long-time volunteer Shirley Sabin wishes that people would focus more on the history of Penniman House instead of on the ghosts. "Some people say that the house is haunted or that there are spirits in the house—depends on who you are talking to." She feels these rumors might have started when it was boarded up for a number of years. "When the park got it, they didn't do anything with it until a grant was funded, and then they decided to restore it." Nor did it help that when the house was used as a temporary residence for park rangers, the rangers and their families began to speak about ghosts inside. "There is a story about a ranger and his wife who were living there," says Sabin, "and they claimed things would happen, nothing bad, just things would get moved, or they would hear things, and then the rumors were 'Oh, it's the Captain. Oh, it's Mrs. Penniman. Oh, it's Bessie.'"

Besides the captain, the second ghost candidate is the captain's wife, Betsey Augusta Knowles Penniman. Adventurous, brave, and loyal, she sailed around the world with her husband, including on a four-year voyage on the whaling bark *Minerva*. "Gustie," the captain's nickname for his wife, took over command when nature and necessity dictated. The Pennimans' daughter, Bessie, wrote of one instance when her mother's navigational skills saved the ship. "When Captain Penniman and most of the crew were ashore off Patagonia, South America, suddenly a tropical storm arose, and the ship was blown one hundred miles out to sea. Under her direction, the *Europa* weathered the storm at sea and returned two days later, with all sails set, to pick up Captain Penniman and his crew."

Whether at sea or on land, Gustie Penniman's good humor, even at her own expense, never faltered. She dared to wear a pair of men's pants, taboo for woman of that era, to help her husband repair the keel of their pleasure sailboat, *Elsie*. To mark the occasion, Gustie penned a poem, "For the Dollar Scrabble."

> I said to earn my dollar,
> I would help my charming spouse,
> But he as quick retorted
> That my place was in the house.
>
> . . .
>
> But I donned a tam "shanter"
> And bloomers neat and natty
> While my daughter was convulsed with glee,
> and my husband called me fatty.

With such a jovial outlook, Gustie's spirit surely appreciates each and every visitor and takes all their comments in stride.

Gustie and Edward Penniman had three children: Eugene, born in 1860; Betsey ("Bessie"), born in 1868; and Edward ("Ned"), born in 1870. They all spent time at sea with their parents. While the boys fared well, Bessie suffered from seasickness. In a letter to his daughter, Captain Penniman acknowledged that life on a whaling ship is not always pleasant:

> Dear Bessie,
> It is a dark stormy day. . . I don't think you would enjoy yourself at sea, and I see by your writing that you don't care to come. You will be much better off going to school . . . than you would on board the *Jacob A. Howland*. . . . We did catch a very large right whale the other day. The *Jacob* does not smell very sweet. I expect you would snuff up your nose if you was here and say she did not smell good . . . Hope this will find you well and happy.
> Papa

Bessie stayed with her aunt in Cambridge, returning home only when her family had safely arrived from exotic ports from the Arctic Ocean to the South Pacific. Bessie is the third possible candidate for the ghost who lives at Penniman House.

The Pennimans' home in Eastham was built on land in the Fort Hill area, where Captain Penniman had grown up. The two-and-a-half-story Second Empire-style structure rises over a raised terrace. From the octagonal cupola, the family could gaze at the Atlantic Ocean and Cape Cod Bay. The Pennimans' granddaughter described the early twentieth century view:

> We had a beautiful view of the town Cove, the ocean and the sand dunes. . . . The sun rising out of the sea was spectacular. We watched whales blow as they swam and cavorted in the water, as seen from our dining room window. Now all that is gone as the trees have been allowed to grow.

At fifty-three, Captain Penniman retired from whaling and settled into the life of a gentleman farmer in his new home, built on twelve acres of land, with barns, greenhouse, orchard, gardens, and outbuildings. The eight-room home was said to be the first on the Cape with indoor plumbing. There was a three-hole outhouse attached to the barn for servants and laborers.

The captain died in 1913, leaving the house to his wife, Gustie. Their sons married and moved on. Daughter Bessie may have never truly left. "Bessie lived there her entire eighty-nine years," explains Sabin. "Bessie never married, never had children." Surrounded by the artifacts her parents had collected—scrimshaw, china tea sets, Cloisonné vases—Bessie, who inherited the house in 1921, clung to the memories, never changing or moving anything from its appointed place. This may explain why some who believe the house has ghosts assume it is Bessie's spirit. Upset that family treasures and mementos are missing and can't be found, the ghostly form of Bessie roams from room to room. Occasional reports surface of a lone female figure carrying a kerosene lamp. She appears in one window and then moves on to the next.

However, while Bessie never had children, she was not childless. Bessie's younger brother, Ned, had three daughters. After the death of his wife, the older girls went to live with other relatives, and the youngest, two-year-old Irma, moved in with her grandparents and aunt. Aunt Bessie raised Irma, who is the fourth possibility for the ghost. Like her Aunt Bessie, Irma developed a strong attachment and protectiveness toward her childhood home.

According to Sabin, who researched the Penniman family history, "Irma lived there with her Aunt Bessie until she married at twenty-one or twenty-two." Irma's first marriage and subsequent divorce is a mystery. "The previous head of the park's Visitor Center interviewed Irma and made a tape. Irma talked about her life, that she had been married in the parlor. It was a short marriage that didn't work out." Sabin is puzzled. "I can't find any records, no marriage certificate in town. I don't know who the man was."

What is known is that by the summer of 1932, Irma was single again and living back at Penniman House. Irma volunteered at Cape Cod's Ornithological Research Station, where she met ornithologist Maurice Broun. Irma, not one for shyness, recognized her soul mate immediately and walked right up to him. "I think it would be great to marry an ornithologist," she said. Irma got her way. "They fell in love," says Sabin, "and Maurice later wrote a book, and he talked about how Irma would go with him to these smelly, dirty rookeries, and how if she could put up with all this and bird banding, then he would band her. So, they married, and he was absolutely the love of her life." Irma became Mrs. Maurice Broun in 1934 and moved with her husband to the Hawk Mountain Sanctuary in Pennsylvania, but Penniman House and Aunt Bessie were always in her thoughts.

Even when Aunt Bessie was living in the house, its outward appearance instilled in visitors a sense of foreboding. In his memoir, *The Autobiography of a Yankee-Nevadan,* George A. Phelps describes the 1944 trip he took with Irma to check up on her elderly aunt, who "lived in the house that belonged to her father, a turn-of-the-century Yankee sea captain who had sailed the seven seas." Phelps says that they arrived on a spooky Halloween night.

> Mist, rising from the nearby bay swirled around us as we walked beneath a Gothic arch, the jawbones of a whale. I shivered, not only because of the chilly night air but also because the place looked as it was haunted. I half expected to be greeted by witches and hobgoblins.

As they approached the front entrance, George's misgivings increased. "With a squeak, the door swung open to reveal a small, gray-haired lady holding a shawl over her sloping shoulders. Aunt Bessie fondly greeted her niece and then held out a thin, pale hand to me." To the uneasy guest, the interior, "looking more a museum than a dwelling," offered little to lessen his discomfort. "There were more foreign artifacts and exotic memorabilia than I'd ever before seen in one place."

Bessie Penniman died at the Penniman House. In her will, she left the house and its contents to the local cemetery association in the hopes that they would continue to care for the Penniman family plot. There was one important proviso—Irma and her husband were to have a lifetime tenancy. Irma, however, was not happy with the arrangement. She approached the cemetery association and, after a prolonged negotiation, purchased the title to Penniman House. Although Irma and Maurice did vacation there, the couple's primary residence remained in Pennsylvania. Irma continued to worry about the future of her childhood home.

The Cape Cod National Seashore was established in 1961. Irma offered the home to them with the idea that it would be opened as a museum. The park service wanted this prime piece of land to save it from development but had little interest in the house—or its contents. "Irma offered to sell the furniture for an additional one hundred dollars a room, which would have been an absolute gold mine," states Sabin. "The man she was dealing with said to her, 'We are not in the antique business.' She was so hurt. This is directly from her mouth because I communicated with her for several years before she died."

Because she could not be there to care for the Penniman House, the sale to the National Park Service went through, and Irma had no other option but to put her family heirlooms on the auction block. For the first time in three generations, the Penniman House would be vacant, boarded up and devoid of life. The rumors of a haunted house on the hill resurfaced.

Maurice Broun, Irma's husband, died of cancer in 1979. To great surprise, Irma soon wed husband number three: Spencer Kahn, Maurice's best man at his wedding to Irma. Once married, Spencer Kahn and Irma Broun moved to Kahn's home in Modesto, California.

After its short stint as temporary housing for park rangers, the National Park Service opened Penniman House to tours on a limited basis. When Shirley and her husband, Ed Sabin, began to volunteer as tour guides, they contacted Irma Penniman Broun Kahn in California. "At the time, very little was known or written down about family. I have a very curious mind, and if we were going to do tours, we needed to learn more."

Irma, widowed once again, invited the Sabins to California for a visit. Irma died a week before their much-anticipated meeting. She was ninety-seven. Irma's accountant called to say that he saw the date of the meeting on the calendar—it was important to Irma, and she would have wanted them notified. "I asked when was the service, and we went," states Sabin. "It was the shortest service I have ever been to in my entire life. Irma had said [to] keep it short, but I don't think she meant that short!"

The accountant shocked the Sabins even further when he asked if they would take Irma's ashes back to the Penniman House and put them on the mantle. "I said, 'I don't think so.'" Sabin just couldn't

The entrance to the Penniman House is through the jawbones of a whale.

imagine Irma's ashes in an urn perched on the fireplace mantel in an empty house. She had a better idea. "I suggested he bury the ashes in the Penniman family plot. In fact, I told him that her name is already on the big headstone along with Maurice's." Sabin added, "If you want to do that, I will arrange a memorial service and write the eulogy." Local family members attended, along with Irma's accountant and a staff member from Hawk Mountain. "So, we had all aspects of her life represented, including representatives of the cemetery association. We buried her ashes. Maurice's had been scattered. We put a stone with Irma's name. She always said she wanted to go home, and home was Eastham, where she grew up."

Three generations of Pennimans—the captain and his wife, Gustie; their children, Eugene, Edward, Bessie; and their granddaughter, Irma Penniman Broun Kahn—lived in and loved the Penniman House. If Capt. Edward Penniman's spirit is watching over the house, Sabin agrees that he would probably be pleased that the National Park is allowing visitors to enter, but "he would want them to keep it in better shape—I am sure that's true." She adds, "I expect he would like to have it furnished, but that is not possible."

One ghost or four? An accurate tally of the spirits of the Penniman House is left to the individual. "I've had strangers come into the house and they'd say that they feel things. The wife of one of our rangers, one of our volunteers, doesn't like to be there. Our curator, who is retired, didn't like to go over there; she didn't like the vibe she gets." Shirley Sabin, the eighty-year-old tour guide, has had no issues with the house and remains a skeptic.

Lagniappe: To find the Penniman House, head towards Eastham on Route 6A. Turn right on Fort Hill Road and follow its serpentine pathway. Drive past the captain's house on the right. The parking lot is at the bottom of the next hill on the left. Climb back up on foot and enter the grounds through the side "gate." Walk beneath the mammoth, bleached-white jaw bones of a sixty-three-foot whale, and you will feel a bit like George Phelps when he arrived on Halloween eve in 1944. The jaws have served as the main entrance since the days of Captain Penniman—a stark reminder of his source of wealth and days at sea.

19

The Obsessive-Compulsive Exhorter

I'm overdue. I'm really in a stew.
Oh dear! Oh, dear!
I shall be too late!
—The White Rabbit, from Lewis Carroll's
Alice's Adventures in Wonderland

Keeping a vigilant eye on every timber, truss, joint, and joist, preacher-in-training Stephen Collins oversaw the building of the first meeting house in Truro. Getting to Sunday service on time became his overriding obsession. In the modern era, Collins might have been diagnosed with obsessive-compulsive disorder. In the eighteenth century, the good people of Truro could only watch and give him a wide berth as he made his mad dash up the Hill of Storms to reach the church. The fate of one small child was sadder still: little Silas Rich died because Collins would not slow down. Filled with repentance, the preacher's spirit forever mourns his disastrous deed.

A dusty, heavily trodden pathway winds its way up a hilltop in Truro. Looming over the hill is a simple rectangular meeting house. Two green doors on either side of the front façade provide the only touch of color to the blinding-white clapboard structure. The meeting house is capped with a squat bell tower that holds an original Paul Revere Foundry bell. The steeple stands as "a memorial to the many brave seafarers and hard-working Cape Cod shipbuilders, chandlers, fishermen, farmers, merchants, and their families." There is no cross on this house of worship. The sole identifying feature is a plaque mounted between the mullioned windows. The inscription states the basic facts.

A distraught spirit on horseback returns over and over to this meeting house.

The plaque on the First Congregational Parish of Truro.

In those first years, Stephen Collins was a passionate "exhorter;" his role was to urge the people to give their lives to God. Those who heard his pleas said that his exhortations were "full of full of fire; his pungent logic carried conviction to the mind." To reach the new house of worship, Collins made the arduous climb up the Hill of Storms on foot. As he grew older and more impatient, the passing of time began to haunt him. To ensure that he would always be the first to arrive at the church, the exhorter acquired a haggard gray mare. The pitiful creature was swaybacked, and the deeply sagging line of her misshapen spine altered her gait. The more Collins urged her forward, the more her abundant flanks flapped from side to side. The sight would have been comical if not for the stress evident in the bulging eyes of both horse and rider.

On the first Sunday of every month, the congregation celebrated Communion Sunday. Collins transported the sacramental wine in a jug suspended on a cord from his saddle horn. As he passed those on foot who were making their way reverently to church, the faithful pleaded with the exhorter to slow down. They feared for their lives—blinded by the ever-present anxiety that he might be late, Collins and his misguided steed could easily trample them to death. The fact that the sacred wine was rapidly sloshing out of the jug was also a source of considerable concern.

On one fateful May Sabbath, fresh spring flowers were laid on the graves in the Burying Acre. Too many of the tombstones had no bodies lying underneath, for the sons of Truro went to sea at age ten, the accepted age for a "first-timer." These youngsters with limited skills often lost their footing, never to be seen again. Still, their grieving mothers insisted on a burial in the Remembering Plot.

Silas Rich barely escaped the same fate. Silas's first and only fishing voyage was on his father's sloop. Without warning, a gale tossed Henry Rich's prized wooden vessel like a child's plaything in seven different directions. Young Silas's foot became entangled in the rigging. As the sloop dipped under yet another bruising wave, Henry's beloved son was dragged overboard. A dazed Silas clung to a splintered spar. The sea gods were with him, and his father was

Townspeople lay fresh flowers on the graves.

The Remembering Plot honors those lost at sea.

able to pull him back on board. But the sea gods exacted a price: Silas suffered a severe blow to the head. He lost his memory, and his gait became worse than that of the exhorter's pitiful horse. The once bright and promising ten-year-old was reduced to the mental state of a toddler, and he hobbled crablike, never again to stand upright.

The community rallied around the stricken child. Tragedy always seemed to follow the fishing fleet: a sailor with gangrene who lost his foot, a mate with a mangled hand, a captain whose brain was addled by too much ale. So the good men, women, and children of Truro did not judge or overly sympathize They accepted Silas for who he had become. If they encountered Silas wandering aimlessly through the village or woods, they took his hand and guided him home. They patiently answered his endless questions about sea, sun, sand, and sky.

Silas loved church. He sat motionless in a trance throughout the service, never causing a disturbance, never restlessly swinging his feet. Silas liked the exhorter, who always had a kind word for the child. On Sundays, Silas would stand by the side of the path and cheer Collins's horse on as he roared up the hill: "Ride on! Ride on!"

That disastrous May Sabbath was Communion day, and Collins was in a particular frenzy. He lashed out at the old gray mare, imploring her to go faster and faster. The leather wine jug beat against her flank. She snorted and wheezed, gasping for breath. Sweat dripped down her mangy forelock into her one good eye. The people wisely stepped aside to let horse and rider pass. Silas, unable to comprehend the danger, placed one crippled foot, then the other, directly in the path of the charging steed. The old mare reared and trampled the boy. Collins felt the impact but did not pull back on the reins. Instead, he reached to steady the jug of wine and kicked his heels sharply into the frightened horse's sides to charge ever forward. His only glancing thought to this callous act was that someone in the community would surely pick the boy back up.

Horse and rider were beyond the realm of reason. They plunged through the Burying Acre, knocking over tombstones, treading on graves, leaving deep gouges in the soft earth, and scattering the fragrant bouquets of flowers laid in memory of lost loved ones.

The Hill of Storms, where the exhorter's horse trampled young Silas.

After nearly crashing into the meeting house door, exhorter Collins clumsily dismounted, leaving the mare free of her master's torment. With the wine jug clutched to his chest, the mad man took his place on the deacon's bench to await the tardy congregation.

Two good men carried the crumpled body of Silas down the center aisle. They laid him gently on the front bench. His parents wept silently. The service commenced. Collins sat and stared at the closed eyes of the small figure. At the conclusion of the service, the distraught exhorter rose to pass down the aisle. He paused and leaned over Silas. Those inside the church turned their heads away.

The obsessive exhorter never entered the church again. On the Sabbath, he would approach the meeting house and stand outside until the service was over, then he would scurry over to the Burying Acre. He knelt for long hours before a fresh grave. Upon his death, the forgiving congregation buried him beside his beloved church.

His tortured spirit, however, cannot rest. On a first Sunday's eve when a full moon graces the night, many locals report that the exhorter's troubled spirit returns, riding a phantom mare. Those intent on making contact with the paranormal claim that the first sounds are the labored wheezing of a horse, then hoofs pounding on soft clay, followed by the splashing of liquid in a container and the creak of worn leather as the phantom rider slowly swings a leg over the saddle. The apparition dismounts and moves with considerable difficulty in starts and stops as if unsure of his way—or his welcome. He kneels at last before a weather-beaten headstone, the inscription illegible to the human eye. His lips move soundlessly. Then, he remounts and disappears into the night.

Today, a host of time-worn gravestones, some bowed as if in prayer, surround the meeting house. Ribbons of orange and rust-colored lichen lend an almost-ghoulish, Halloween appearance where the fungus creeps over the stones. Acid rain, wind, freezes, and thaws, along with the algae and mold, have reduced the incised inscriptions on many headstones to faint blurs. The graves of poor little Silas Rich and the compulsive preacher who trampled him with his horse are concealed within the ancient cemetery.

An ancient tombstone whose name is lost to time.

Concealed in the cemetery are the graves of Silas and the obsessive-compulsive exhorter.

Lagniappe: Haunted tales often carve their own path through history. Yet, just as often in the retelling of the story, there are glimmers of facts shining through the legend. In 1884, Simeon D. Hamilton Hurd compiled a history of Plymouth County, Massachusetts, which at the time included Cape Cod. Hurd describes the oldest religious edifice in Truro where exhorter Collins may still pay his respects on his haunted ride.

> From all the facts in the case, we conclude that the first meeting house was on . . . the hill of storms . . . as a beacon for the tempest-tossed mariner. After several years of disuse, it was taken down. . . . In 1827 a new church edifice was erected at Truro village, southwest of the old meeting house, and in which the present distinctive Congregational society worships and claims to be a continuation of the old. The old burying ground with its first head stone of 1713 remains to mark the site of the first meeting house and first laid-out ground of Truro. . . .

The local exhorter was a prominent factor in the life of the primitive church, and with these the Truro society was well supplied. Ephraim Doane Rich, Ebenezer L. Davis, Stephen Collins and others will not be forgotten for their good works . . . the logic of these plain men was incontrovertible, although presented in a rude and uncultivated manner . . . earnestness, and perhaps eccentricity were marked in their labors.

Massachusetts Vital Records for 1849 list a Capt. Stephen Collins, born January 28, 1782, who died July 29, 1861. He was the father of twelve, six girls and six boys. Collins participated in the religious community of Cape Cod. There is no record that this Collins trampled Silas Rich to death on his way to church. However, the legend of his infamous deed and his paranormal visits to the grave of his victim lives on in the oral history of the Cape.

The Provincetown library, home to the Rose Dorothea.

20

A Clean Sweep

The *Rose Dorothea* rides under full sail on the second floor of the Provincetown library. The schooner measures sixty-six feet six inches long, and her forty-eight-foot main mast skims the third floor ceiling. She is the largest indoor boat model of her kind and has one other notable distinction: the *Rose Dorothea* is skippered by a phantom captain.

The Provincetown library occupies a stunning 1860s-era edifice on Commercial Street. In the third-floor loft, a library patron works diligently at his laptop. On a clear summer day, the towering windows offer an expansive view, stretching some fifteen miles over the harbor and bay, but the eyes of graduate student John never veer from his computer monitor. After two grueling hours, John allows himself a short break. He removes his black, wire-frame reading glasses and lays them over the keyboard. He pinches the bridge of his nose and rubs his eyes. Mid-rub, he freezes and then slowly rotates his shoulders clockwise to stare down at the deck of the *Rose Dorothea*. With his head cocked slightly, John appears to be listening. The silence is broken abruptly by his loud laughter. A librarian, pushing a cart stacked with books past the hull, frowns in disapproval. Waving his hand in acknowledgement of his transgression, John mouths a perfunctory "I'm sorry."

When asked what made him laugh so hard, John is unabashed. "I just can't help it. When I hear the sweep—the *swish, swish, swish* of that broom—I mean, what more of a motivator can you ask for? It's as if he knows I need a push to get to the finish line." John is quick to clarify. "It's Captain Perry, of course—his spirit, anyway.

The bow of the replica of the Rose Dorothea *under the third-floor loft.*

A phantom captain sweeps the deck with a phantom broom.

John underscores the connection between himself and the former captain of the *Rose Dorothea.* "I know it could seem strange listening for ghosts and ghost brooms in a library, but ever since I started coming here to work on my master's thesis about sailing vessels in New England waters, well, I'm just aware he's here, and he approves, and it's his way of helping."

Capt. Marion Perry is hailed as the winner of the 1907 Fisherman's Cup sailing race, a forty-two-mile dash between Boston to Gloucester and back also known as the Lipton Cup. As his fishing schooner crossed the finish line, Captain Perry is said to have grabbed a broom and "swept the deck clean," a symbolic gesture of having beaten his rival, the *Jessie Costa,* captained by Manuel Costa. During the June 25, 1988, dedication ceremony for the replica of the *Rose Dorothea,* a Portuguese man, boat builder Francis "Flyer" Santos, also grabbed a broom and "swept the deck" in emulation of Captain Perry, who brought fame to his homeport of Provincetown.

The original *Rose Dorothea* was a Grand Banks fishing schooner with a rounded Indian Head bow that enabled her to sail closer to the wind, making her faster than other schooners of her era. Built in 1905 at a cost of $15,000, she measured just more than 108 feet in length. The captain named her for his lovely wife.

The library's replica clearly honors Captain Perry's victory, but it is just a showpiece. Her hull gleams in the sunlight with a glossy coat of black paint. Not a speck of dirt mars her pristine, white deck. Her name glistens in gold script on her bow. It would be reasonable to question why Captain Perry's ghost would haunt a replica rather than his actual ship.

The schooner met a horrific end. Sold in 1910 to a local fishing captain, six years later she was sold again to a Newfoundland company that used her to ferry salt and supplies to Portugal. In February 1917, a German submarine surfaced next to the schooner. After allowing her crew to evacuate in dories, the U-boat sank her. This once-valiant fishing vessel disintegrated at the bottom of the sea off the coast of Portugal. So, with nothing left of his ship to command, Captain Perry's invincible spirit seems to have chosen the library's magnificent half-scale model to relive his victory in the great Fisherman's Cup race.

The race began on August 1, 1907, in Boston. The *Rose Dorothea* and the *Jessie Costa,* another Provincetown schooner, battled to steal the wind from the other's sails. A third vessel, the *James W. Parker,* reputedly with a band on board, lagged behind. As the *Rose Dorothea* and the *Jessie Costa* rounded Gloucester for the return leg back to Boston, the rising wind and seas pushed the boats faster, "heeling them over so their rails were tipped to the water line." Approaching the final mark, the crew of the *Rose Dorothea* heard a sharp crack. The foretopmast had snapped in the middle, leaving its sail to dangle uselessly. The jubilant crew of the *Jessie Costa* was eager to take advantage of their competitor's disaster—but fate and skillful sailing intervened. Without its jib topsail, the *Rose Dorothea* could point higher into the wind and sail a straighter course. The *Jessie Costa* had to tack more often. The *Rose Dorothea,* minus its foretopmast, crossed the finish line two minutes and thirty-four seconds ahead of its closest competitor. As she entered Boston harbor, Captain Perry grabbed a broom, swept the deck clean, and celebrated with a flourish. If the captain's spirit is still at it, who can blame him? The library is accessible to all, and sometimes even ghosts appreciate a little attention.

Captain Perry's prize was $650 and the Lipton Cup, a three-foot-tall sterling-silver trophy. Presenting the Lipton Cup to the sea captain was then-mayor of Boston John F. "Honey Fitz" Fitzgerald, the grandfather of Pres. John F. Kennedy and United States senators Robert "Bobby" Kennedy and Edward "Ted" Kennedy.

Perry brought the Lipton Cup back to Provincetown, where today it has a place of honor inside the library's main entrance. A majestic eagle perches on top of the ornate trophy. A pair of winged seahorses serves as handles. Other symbols of the sea—embossed sea shells, whimsical fish—adorn the sides. In 1980, the trophy was stolen and held for a $2,000 ransom. The bumbling thief was already a suspect in several similar crimes, and the Lipton Cup soon was recovered from where it had been hastily stashed in nearby sand dunes. After a thorough cleaning, it was back on display with the engraving on the ebony base proclaiming: "Presented by Sir Thomas Lipton, 1907, and won by the schooner *Rose Dorothea.*"

Who was this knighted British gentleman, and why would he sponsor a race between fishermen in Massachusetts waters?

Having made three failed attempts to win the coveted America's Cup for Great Britain, this millionaire mogul of tea fame earned the title of "World's Best Loser." Sir Thomas Lipton sought to redeem himself, and he was not above a bit of clever marketing. The founder of the Lipton Tea Company, he was involved with branding before branding ever entered the advertising lexicon. Tired of racing fabulously expensive pleasure yachts owned by like-minded gentlemen, Sir Thomas looked for a new diversion. Intrigued by the speed and seaworthiness of New England's commercial fishing fleet, he offered a custom-made trophy to the winner of a coastal race where "winds were unpredictable, and sail and helm handling were crucial elements to success." The Lipton Cup featured enameled flags of the United States and England. A closer look reveals a smaller flag with a green shamrock in the center, a crafty way of incorporating the flags of Lipton's three *Shamrock*s, the yachts which Lipton had sailed in pursuit of his thwarted America's Cup dream.

When Lipton first approached Perry about participating in the Fisherman's Race, the frugal captain declined. The price of fish was soaring, and a frivolous sailing race held little appeal. However, the captain's wife, Rose Dorothea, who "favored nice things," had a different agenda. Once she glimpsed the extravagant trophy, she knew that the only proper place for it was on her parlor mantel. The big, barrel-chested captain, sporting a reputation as the "best fish-killer" in the fleet, acquiesced to the desire of his wife. With her husband's amazing win, Rose Dorothea's mantel had a shiny new centerpiece, and Provincetown's seafaring reputation as the best of the best was secured.

In the early 1900s, Provincetown remained primarily a fishing village. The victory made Perry a local hero, allowed the largely

Portuguese population to "rise above the ethnic slurs flung their way," and erased the smug superiority of nearby Gloucester, which was known for building fast fishing schooners. It also one-upped Boston, where society's elite raced yachts that often cost more than an entire fishing crew made in its lifetime.

The *Provincetown (MA) Advocate*, a local newspaper, touted the triumphant homecoming of Captain Perry aboard the *Rose Dorothea:* "Volleys were fired from small arms by men stationed at intervals along the route . . . [the] good-natured crowd voiced their approval in cheers for the skillful captain, his doughty crew, and the trim hull that successfully fought for the grandest racing trophy known in fishing annals the world over."

Given the impact of the race on his hometown, his pride in his Portuguese heritage, and the admiration of his wife, it is understandable that Capt. Marion Perry's ghost still has an itch to gloat. This is, after all, the ghost of a man who, when Pres. Theodore Roosevelt was in Boston and wanted to meet the Lipton Cup winner, is reported to have responded: "Tell the President if he wants to see me, he knows where he can find me!"

For patrons of the Provincetown library such as graduate student John, it's not hard to find the captain's steadfast spirit. Those believers are just as certain that the *swish, swish, swish* of the phantom broom across the deck of the reborn *Rose Dorothea* is the captain's little reminder to steer for the stars.

Lagniappe: There are some interesting questions about this entire situation: What is a ship's model of this magnitude doing inside a library, and how did it get there in the first place? The current Provincetown library began life as the Center Methodist Episcopal Church. At its completion in 1860, it was the largest church building of the Methodist denomination anywhere in the United States. It eventually proved to be too big for the congregation, and in 1958, the Methodists sold the church with its one-hundred-foot spire to Walter P. Chrysler Jr. for an art museum. The venture failed, as did a 1974 attempt to create a "Center for the Arts." On

The deck of the replica with its phantom captain and broom.

Ovals were cut into the ceiling to accommodate the masts.

July 4, 1976, it reopened as the Provincetown Heritage Museum. The museum's board needed an attraction that would be a tourist draw, and a model of the *Rose Dorothea* fulfilled their vision of the ultimate symbol of Provincetown's glory days of sailing and fishing. Master boat builder Francis "Flyer" Santos, the grandson of one of the original crew, was hired to build a half-scale replica. Mimicking the model-ship-in-a bottle technique, Santos constructed the *Rose Dorothea* replica from the hull up using the former second-floor church sanctuary as a permanent dry dock. Though half scale, the replica's size required a few structural modifications to the building.

Ovals were cut into the ceiling to accommodate the height of the masts. The special glass doors of the aptly named Bowsprit Reading Room (the former choir loft) were designed to allow the ship's protruding bowsprit to point towards the harbor. The exacting process took eleven years. On June 25, 1988, the completed model was dedicated to the fishermen of Provincetown and their remarkable

The library repurposed church pews for their bookshelves.

sailing schooners. By 2000, as museum visitors declined, use of the old Provincetown library increased, and the collections of the two institutions merged. The *Rose Dorothea,* the victorious fishing schooner, remains the soaring centerpiece of the library. Bookshelves in the form of waves follow the curve of the hull. To pay homage to the building's ecclesiastical origins, mahogany arm rests from the former church pews are now decorative caps for display shelves on the first floor. The church bells in the belfry still ring—instead of calling congregants to prayer, they announce the daily opening of the library doors and the opportunity to view the *Rose Dorothea,* whose phantom captain stands alert at the helm to inspire and encourage.

21

Noepe, the Enchanted Isle

*It's a special, insular, quiet, healing, glorious place. . . . There's a strange
continuity to life on the Vineyard.*
— Mike Wallace, *60 Minutes* news correspondent

Ribbons of gray fog curl over the multicolored clay cliffs near
Aquinnah on Martha's Vineyard. The Wampanoag people smile, for
they know it as the smoke from Maushop's pipe, a sign that his spirit

The Aquinnah cliffs of Martha's Vineyard, the Enchanted Isle.

is still among them. This legendary giant created Vineyard Sound to protect his tribe from the fighting on the mainland. The Wampanoags, "People of the First Light," called their island home "Noepe," the land amid the streams.

As the new people began to arrive in the mid-seventeenth century, the lives of the Wampanoags were forever changed. In 1642, there were 3,000 Wampanoag tribal members living on the island. By 1764, that number had dropped to 313.

English explorer Bartholomew Gosnold is credited as the first European to sight the island in 1602; he named it Martha's Vineyard. It is thought he chose the name "Martha" in memory of his second daughter, who died in infancy, and "Vineyard" for its abundance of wild grapes. In the archives of the Royal Danish Library in Copenhagen, there are documents that allude to Vikings who sighted the island six hundred years before the English and called it "Vinland."

The first English settlement was established in 1642 at Great Harbor, now Edgartown. The island's oldest surviving residence is the Vincent House, tucked behind the Fisher House on Main Street. A gauzy female apparition doesn't know what to make of the house's current location.

Dwarfed by the mammoth Greek Revival Old Whaling Church and the palatial Dr. Daniel Fisher House, the simple, gray-shingled, three-room Vincent House looks out of place. Donated in 1977 to the Martha's Vineyard Preservation Trust by the MacKenty and Bigelow families, it was moved from its original location on the shore of the Edgartown Great Pond to Main Street to be used as a museum depicting early island life.

A workman making repairs to the foundation of the Old Whaling Church ambles over to the Vincent House. "It's closed for the season, you know." He wipes his hands on a rag hanging from his back pocket and peers around the corner of the entrance ell that juts off to the side. "My brother-in-law used to come here to help out with the landscaping, mostly mowing. He won't come here no more." The workman sniffs at the air and lowers his voice as if embarrassed

A confused ghost runs in and out of the doors of the Vincent House.

to be telling tales. "Mike, that's my brother-in-law, said when he'd get here early in the morning, well, he'd see this woman, a figure I guess, and she'd come out of that door right there, go around the house, and go back in the door on the other side." The workman reaches for the rag in his pocket and wipes his hands again. "'Course, the doors were closed like they are now, locked, and Mike said this woman in old-fashioned clothes acts like she doesn't know where she is. She checks out the big house and the church, then runs back inside, scared like." Having disclosed as much as he cares to share, the workman rejoins the group digging under the foundation of the Old Whaling Church.

According to the historic plaque mounted to the left of the entrance door, the Vincent House was built in 1672 by William Vincent, but the attached entrance ell is thought to be the lone surviving element of a house that overlooked Great Pond in 1638. The mysterious female phantom could be an early-morning illusion, a shape morphing from the fog that often shrouds the island, or a lost soul bewildered by her new surroundings.

The disconcerted lady is not the only phantom on the island. On Water Street in Edgartown, entrepreneur John Daggett established a tavern to accommodate thirsty settlers. His business acumen came into question in 1660, when he was fined five shillings for "selling strong liquor." Despite the setback, his tavern flourished. By the 1750s, the Daggett House had grown in size, also serving as a sailor's boarding house, store, customs house, and, during the whaling era, counting house. By the mid-twentieth century, as tourism took over the island, the Daggett House emerged as a popular inn—its harbor location and rumors of ghosts were a big draw.

The thirty-one guest rooms and suites offer spacious accommodations, with one cramped exception. (The owners promoted the "cozy" room as a "romantic retreat.") The Secret Staircase Room could only be accessed by pulling a hinged bookcase away from the wall and ascending a narrow staircase. Most couples were thrilled to have an intimate hidden gem as their own—provided they could tolerate little phantoms at play.

When the house was still a private residence, two little boys lived at the Daggett House with their parents. The older of the two was leaving to visit his grandmother and decided to play a prank. He locked his younger sibling's dog in the room behind the bookcase. He left and told no one. The younger brother went out in the cold, wet night looking for his beloved pet, caught pneumonia, and died. The dog, locked up, died of starvation. On returning from his grandmother's house and learning what had happened, the older brother threw himself in the harbor and drowned.

The siblings made peace with each other in the afterlife, and their laughter is often heard behind the bookcase. The ghost children like to play hide-and-seek with their dog. A truly strange photo taken by a startled visitor shows the hazy image of a little boy and his dog crouched in the beehive-shaped hearth of the old tavern. To appease the whimpering spirit of the deceased dog, members of the housekeeping staff were known to leave dog treats at the foot of the staircase.

Two young phantom brothers and the dog play inside the Daggett House.

In the summer of 2003, a woman named Margaret booked the secret room for herself and her husband to celebrate their tenth wedding anniversary. "We stayed in the Secret Staircase Room. It was fun going behind the fake bookcase in the dining area and sneaking up to our own private getaway. At night we kept hearing what sounded like two little boys chasing each other around the room. We didn't mind them, but after a while the barking dog got to be too much." Margaret's review came with a warning. "If you are looking for a romantic night with your husband, don't come here. These ghosts are noisy."

In 2014, the Daggett House, after years as an inn, is once again a private residence, where hopefully, two little boys and their pet still have a place to play.

Edgartown on Martha's Vineyard rose to some prominence as a center of the whaling industry. Successful sea captains built magnificent mansions along the waterfront. The Victorian Inn, a

A sea captain prowls the rooms of the Victorian Inn.

A guest had a ghostly dialogue with the captain on the staircase.

short stroll from the Daggett House on South Water Street, was once the home of Capt. Lafayette Rowley. Owners Stephen and Karyn Caliri do not market the inn as a haunted house, but several of their guests have claimed to have had encounters with spirits during their stay.

"One woman swore she had a dialogue with Lafayette Rowley on the staircase at night, and they chatted up a storm." Karyn indicates the carpeted staircase with its richly stained balustrade in the front hall that leads to the second- and third-floor guest suites. "We had another guest, a man, insist he put his night slippers beside the bed, and when he got up in the morning, they were moved." A female guest described the ghost as "amorous," reaching out and touching her as she slept.

The "incident" that really grabbed Karyn and Stephen's attention involved a couple staying on the third floor. "They came down for breakfast and said a loud crash woke them up in the middle of the night. They described a heavy thud, like a bureau falling over, but all the furniture in their room remained upright." Karyn is momentarily distracted. She aligns a book with its mate on the black marble mantel in the parlor. "I don't know. They were very convincing. Both of them told the same story. Stephen went to the third floor and looked everywhere. He even went up on the roof, thinking a big tree limb might have fallen, but nothing." The innkeeper sneaks a glance at the small oval portrait of a scowling Captain Rowley in the parlor.

"The woman who owned the house before us had the house cleansed because she said spooky things happened to her and her guests. She attributed it all to when Lafayette Rowley lived here." Karyn backtracks a little more. "In the beginning, when we first got here, funny things happened, and I did think, 'Oh, my God, there really is a ghost.'" The innkeeper laughs at her own foolishness and dismisses the idea. "The house is not haunted. We are very grounded people. We live here all year long, and nothing has really happened to us."

Out in the courtyard, Karyn's husband is raking leaves from the patio, making final preparations before closing the inn for the season. An accomplished storyteller, Stephen willingly shares what he knows about the sea captain who built his dream home on the island. "When Rowley was still a young cabin boy, his captain and first mate died on the voyage, and he was given command of the ship because he could navigate. He was one of three brothers, all sailors, but he was the only whaler." Stephen puts the rake down and walks over to the white picket fence. "That's why I have the carvings of all these whales mounted here—humpbacks, right whales, sperm whales—Captain Rowley went for all of them."

The innkeeper also went searching for a portrait of Lafayette Rowley to hang in the home where he had lived with his wife and children. "I found this old poster with the faces and a list of names of one hundred and ten whaling captains from Edgartown." The Edgartown library had the original glass negative, and Stephen ordered an eight-by-ten copy of the young, handsome captain before commissioning a larger portrait. "I was going to have it put in a big gold frame in the parlor." When the copy was delivered, he was in shock. Staring back at him was a stern, foreboding face. "I am looking at an Abraham Lincoln lookalike. I march the guy who made the copy over to the poster and point out who I think is Captain Rowley, and he says, 'Read right to left, not left to right.' . . . When you read right to left, he's got the right captain, the old guy, the Lincoln lookalike." The innkeeper had to rethink his initial idea of a large, framed portrait for guests to admire. "We didn't want to blow him up and make it too creepy around here. Consequently, Captain Rowley stays small."

Karyn and Stephen Caliri have been pleased to host Rowley's relatives. "His great-grandson honeymooned here, and his great-great grandchildren stayed with us." When asked if any of these relatives felt their ancestor's presence in the house, Stephen laughs and replies, "The one on the honeymoon, not so much. You don't do a lot of talking to someone on their honeymoon. The other family came with two kids, so they were a little preoccupied as well, but the wife was really tickled to be in the house and see the picture of her great-grandfather."

Capt. Lafayette Rowley scowls from his portrait in the parlor.

When ghost hunters arrive to check out the inn's haunted status, the innkeepers are tolerant but amused. "We've had people come here with little machines and walk around and announce, 'This room is haunted,' or that room. I am a psychiatrist. When people tell me they are seeing things, I refer them to therapy or get them some medication. If they ask me if I have seen anything, I say, 'No, I take my medication daily.'" For guests who assume that the captain's ghost rises from the nearby cemetery to prowl about the house, Stephen Caliri's sense of humor is evident. "I have been here twenty years, and I have never met anyone who stayed here and didn't pay."

Despite a little jaded skepticism, the gingerbread wonder that is the Victorian Inn may still be the home base for the ghost of Captain Rowley as well as an ideal spot for current visitors to venture forth and explore the legends, lore, and haunted tales of this enchanted isle.

Within the one-hundred-square-mile, triangle-shaped land mass,

246 THE HAUNTING OF CAPE COD AND THE ISLANDS

the towns and villages of Martha's Vineyard—Vineyard Haven, Oak Bluffs, West Tisbury, Chilmark, Aquinnah, and Edgartown, along with the nearby island of Chappaquiddick—allow the past to thrive in the present, just as the smoke from Maushop's pipe drifts over her sandy shores.

Lagniappe: The Martha's Vineyard Preservation Trust manages many of the island's historic landmarks: the Vincent House, the Old Whaling Church, the Dr. Daniel Fisher House, the Chappy Schoolhouse, Alley's General Store, and the Flying Horses Carousel, the nation's oldest platform carousel, which has operated in Oak Bluffs since 1884. Each possesses a certain magic. The Aquinnah Cultural Center depicts the lives of the Wampanoag people, the original first families of the island of Noepe. In the Wampanoag creation story, the giant Maushop lay down on Cape Cod to take a nap. When he awoke, his moccasins were full of sand. He picked each up and flung the sand into the ocean, creating the islands of Martha's Vineyard and Nantucket.

22

The Far Away Land

People talk about ghosts on Nantucket, and that may be a kind of a manifestation of the sense that on this very confined space, there are forces that come to us from around the world, and they come to the vortex of this little island.

—Rick Burns, *Nantucket*

The Wampanoags lived undisturbed on *Nantocke* (the far away land) until 1641, when English authorities deeded the island to Thomas Mayhew and his son. Mayhew sold the island to a group of investors

The sandy shores of the mystical island of Nantocke.

for "the sum of thirty Pounds . . . and also two beaver hats, one for myself and one for my wife." Herman Melville wrote about Nantucket's whaling dominance in *Moby Dick,* and two of his characters—Ahab and Starbuck—were both from the island. Shaped like a half moon, Nantucket was nicknamed the "Little Grey Lady of the Sea" because the island appears to rise from the fog-bound ocean. When navigating Nantucket's cobblestoned streets, the past comes alive and tugs at the present.

In the heart of the historic district, the Roberts House Inn, complete with a wide front porch and wicker furniture, is filled with an abundance of charm, character, and a dash of ghostly ambiance. Three of the four buildings that comprise the Roberts House complex are regular stops on the Nantucket ghost tour circuit.

Sitting on a stool behind the front desk, operations manager Pam Roehm is reluctant to talk about the ghosts of the Roberts House Inn. A maintenance man slings a canvas pouch overflowing with assorted tools over his shoulder and walks down the narrow hallway. Roehm tracks him with her eyes and waits for him to pass. She fidgets with the square brochures in their holder, and then clears her throat before admitting that she has heard about the apparition of a young woman with long hair, clad in a nightgown, appearing in the cellar.

The operations manager is more comfortable describing the buildings and the layout of the rooms. "Where we are is the Roberts' house, built in 1846. Right behind us is the Old Quaker Meeting House. Across the courtyard are the Manor House and our newest property, the Gate House. They're all connected."

The phone rings. Roehm swivels on her stool to answer and enter the reservation in the computer. She swivels back to face the front desk. Her long white pony tail swings in a graceful arc as she returns to the subject of ghosts.

"There are shops on the ground floor of the Old Quaker Meeting House next door. We have rooms on the second floor. There were people staying in room 209. They were asleep, and then they heard this kinda . . . one-way dialogue: 'Mrs. Williams? But, Mrs. Williams—' It was if someone else was in the room arguing, imploring another lady they couldn't see.

The Roberts House Inn has a ghost in the cellar.

"The second time the woman and her husband or her partner heard this ghostly voice call out, they were so shocked they didn't even try talking back to her. They came down in the morning and asked was there a Mrs. Williams who used to live here. And I said, 'I just don't know.' After they left I went down and talked to Michael O'Reilly, who owned the building at the time.

"Michael said to me, 'Isn't that interesting . . . There was a Mrs. Williams who owned a house on this property.' He knew that because he had done research when he first purchased the inn."

The operations manager shares her knowledge of Nantucket history: "The Great Fire of 1846 wiped out one-third of downtown, about three hundred buildings were gone, ashes—none of this existed. Everything you see here was built after 1846." Based on the information she acquired from the previous owner, Roehm adds, "As it turns out, there was a house here before the Old Quaker Meeting House was built, and that's where Mrs. Williams lived." Roehm leans over the desk to make sure her point is understood. "But I hadn't told these guests anything. As a matter of fact, I didn't even know about Mrs. Williams until I talked to Michael."

The Old Quaker Meeting House, which replaced the burnt ruins of Mrs. Williams's house, is also where members of the Society of Friends held religious services. The practices of the Quakers must have been shocking to the staid Puritans of Nantucket. Quakers refused to take oaths, recognize established churches, or recognize the use of a minister, an intermediary to commune with the "Inner Light," the spirit of God. John Richardson, who witnessed Quaker elder Mary Starbuck at one of the meetings, gave a vivid account. "She spoke trembling . . . then she arose, and I observed that she and as many as could well be seen, were wet with Tears from their Faces to the fore-skirts of their Garments and the floor was as though there was a Shower of Rain upon it."

For the next forty years, as their numbers increased, members of the Society of Friends met in a series of buildings such as the Old

One ghost argues with another at the Old Meeting House.

Quaker Meeting House. Empathic guests, staying in the second-floor guest rooms above the shops, claim to feel some of that lingering fervor. Luckily, none have reported any indoor rain showers or a floor "wet from tears."

Roehm has now warmed up to the topic of ghosts. "We've also had people staying in the Manor House in the two rooms on the third floor who said they felt a presence, and their door opened and closed by itself." A workman reported seeing a female figure in the window of the Manor House. The sighting of the Manor House ghost occurred when Michael O'Reilly was having renovation work done in the late 1970s prior to opening the historic building to guests. The workman had securely locked the empty building for the evening only to be shocked on his return to see a woman looking down at him from a second floor window.

The entire complex takes its name from the third owner. William Hussey built the main house facing India Street as a private family

The Manor House ghost peers from the window.

residence. In 1883, his daughter Ann inherited the house and turned it into an inn. In 1889, John Roberts purchased it, and also acquired the Quaker Meeting House around the corner on Center Street. Roberts' daughters continued the innkeeper tradition through the 1960s when the O'Reilly family took over. Michael O'Reilly later expanded the operation with the addition of the 1846 Greek Revival Manor House. Despite diligent research, the only ghost with a name at any of the inn's buildings is the illusive Mrs. Williams.

Open year-round, the Roberts House Inn complex with its varied history attracts a steady stream of admirers captivated by its charm and the opportunity to have a chance encounter with a resident ghost. "We even got a letter from a couple who wanted to book a 'haunted' room and bring equipment to see if we had ghosts." The operations manager flashes a smile. "I don't know how that works."

The Roberts House Inn does not have an exclusive when it comes to ghostly apparitions on Nantucket. A short stroll away, the ghost of Jared Coffin hangs out in the house he built in 1845 wondering why he could never seem to please his wife.

In 1830, Jared built the Moors End, a lovely home on Pleasant Street, then on the outermost edges of the town of Nantucket. Mrs. Coffin had other ideas and said the house was too far out for her taste. So, Jared tried again. In 1845, the couple moved into a new house in the center of town on Broad Street. The elegant, three-story, Federal-style, red-brick mansion was the first of its kind on the island. Less than a year later, Jared's persnickety wife wanted out—the entire island was too remote. The prosperous shipping magnate bowed to his wife's demands for city life, and they moved to Boston.

In 1847, the Nantucket Steamboat Company purchased Jared's home and leased it to managers Mr. and Mrs. Robert Parker, who operated it as an inn called the Ocean House. Herman Melville stayed at the Ocean House with his father-in-law when visiting the island populated by legendary whaling captains after he wrote *Moby Dick*. By 1872, the popular establishment had entertained as many as seventeen hundred guests during the season. In 1874, President and Mrs. Ulysses S. Grant spent an enjoyable week there. With the

The ghost of Jared Coffin wonders why his wife never liked it there.

exception of the World War II years, when it was taken over by the
Coast Guard, the historic landmark has continued to operate as a
resort hotel. In 1961, the Nantucket Historical Trust completely
restored Jared Coffin's home.

An October 2009 article in the *New York Daily News* chronicled
the spookiest hotels to stay in on All Hallows Eve. The article highly
recommended the Jared Coffin House as a place to "hunker down
for a good haunting . . . a hotel where guests checked in a long time
ago, but still refuse to leave." A little girl ghost makes repeated visits
to room 609. A woman who checked in with her mother said that
from the time they arrived, she had an "unsettled feeling." She
described the room as "creepy." During the night, "a small, cold
finger kept poking me in my face." Guests staying in room 223
complain that even with the air conditioning off, the room is frigid
in the heat of the summer. When cold blasts of air sweep through the
room, the phenomenon is attributed to the arrival of a phantom
spirit. The bevy of apparitions also includes a "matron," who might
have served as head housekeeper in the early days of the inn. "Phoebe"
has strict standards. She does not approve of unmarried couples

sleeping in the same bed. The intimidating ghost pulls off their covers and glares at them from the foot of the bed.

Often, when the identity of a particular ghost is known, he or she is described as having a disposition similar to when they were alive. At his wife's insistence, Jared Coffin left his island home, the envy of so many other Nantucket residents. No longer bound in the afterlife to do his wife's bidding, Jared has returned. His favorite spot remains the rocking chair in front of the fireplace. Guests at the Jared Coffin House inn swear the chair rocks by itself, especially at night. Unable to make his wife happy on Nantucket, the accommodating ghost of Jared Coffin must surely beam at the sight of his name in inscribed in gold lettering across the top of the front portico of his dream home.

The diminutive island of Nantucket is 14 miles long and 3½ miles wide, and its ghosts seem intent on maintaining a hold over every square inch. In 1709, George Bunker built a house at 36 Fair Street. Until recently, owner Dexter Tutein operated the residence as the Woodbox Inn. Ghost sightings were a regular occurrence. The staff spoke of the apparitions of a sea captain skulking about; an older,

One of the haunted bedrooms at the Jared Coffin House.

Three ghosts linger at the former Woodbox Inn.

The ghost of the Sherburne Inn locks the doors.

heavy-set woman in all black in the dining room; and an adorable girl ghost who liked to keep them company when they were working.

At the Sherburne Inn on Gay Street, a figure of a woman with red hair in an elegant Victorian gown has a habit of locking the doors. The owners can't figure out if she is trying to lock everyone in or keep intruders out.

It matters little to Nantucket's ghosts if a welcome sign is out or not—the "far away land" will always be their home.

Lagniappe: Over the years, the "Little Grey Lady of the Sea" has developed her own style. Gray-shingled cottages are synonymous with island architecture. "Roof walks," the local term for widow's walks, could have been used as lookouts for ships returning home, but on the island, these rooftop platforms primarily were built for fire prevention. Buckets of sand were kept on the roof walks to put out chimney fires. The Jared Coffin House acted as a firewall in the Great Fire of 1846. As flames devoured the town's wooden structures, the house that Jared built of stalwart brick walls and slate roof didn't burn and curtailed the spread of the catastrophic blaze.

Although Jared Coffin's surname has a macabre connotation, the Coffins of Nantucket proudly trace their lineage to Tristram Coffin, one of the first English settlers on the island. It wasn't until the sixteenth century that "coffin" in English meant a receptacle for the dead. In Old French, the word "cofin" meant basket. Before the arrival of the English, the Wampanoag people wove baskets for utilitarian purposes. By the eighteenth and nineteenth centuries, the islands' sailors and lighthouse keepers began to develop a distinctive basket design. Nantucket baskets in the present day are collectible souvenirs and showpieces, often with handles and lids secured with bone, ivory, or scrimshaw.

Nantucket was considered the whaling capital of the world from 1800 to 1840. Nantucket is an island, county, and town, the only place in America with the same name for all, as well as an inviting locale to seek out a few haunted sights.

23

The Pirate and His Would-Be Bride

Two pale figures walk the beach, arms entwined—two lovers, blissfully reunited. From a different perspective, the same male and female apparitions appear locked in a fierce struggle, a pair of angry wraiths driven by revenge. This is a ghostly tale with conflicting outcomes. The legend of the pirate Samuel Bellamy and the elusive Maria Hallett is as controversial today as it was in the spring of 1717 when Bellamy's ship wrecked on the cruel and unforgiving Wellfleet shoals.

Historic records confirm that "Black Sam" Bellamy was a real pirate, not a fictional character. His exploits are well documented. Born in 1689 near Plymouth, in Devonshire, England, his mother, Elizabeth Pain Bellamy, died shortly after Sam's birth. As a young boy, he snuck out to the bustling wharves, captivated by the privateers unloading their wares. Some of Sam's relatives had immigrated to the American colonies and settled in Eastham in Cape Cod, and he joined them in 1714. The unemployed twenty-five-year-old spent his idle hours at the tavern of distant relative Israel Cole on Great Island, across from Wellfleet harbor. The tavern's patrons were a mixed lot: fisherman, whalers, and traders. The tavern was reputed to be a front for a clandestine warehouse where smuggled and stolen goods were bought, stored, and sold, thus evading the bothersome taxes due the English crown.

In the summer of 1715, news of the wreck of a flotilla of Spanish ships off the Florida coast swept through the tavern. The dozen-plus ships, en route to Spain from Havana, carried a cargo of gold coins and bars and chests of silver, emeralds, pearls, and Chinese porcelain.

The ghosts of Maria and Sam—lovers or angry wraiths? (Photograph by Russell Sillery)

Now, this treasure littered the ocean floor in shallow waters—and penniless Sam fantasized about getting his hands on it.

That summer, Sam was also fantasizing about a beautiful young Eastham girl. While there were unsubstantiated rumors that Sam had abandoned a wife and child back in England, here on the lower Cape, Sam's eye settled on Maria Hallett. The most popular version of their initial encounter holds that Maria was sitting in an orchard under a floating white cloud of apple blossoms. Like Eve tempting Adam, the beautiful maiden held forth an apple. The youthful enchantress is described as having hair that "glistened like corn silk at suncoming," and eyes "the color of hyacinth." Reading almost like a modern-day bodice-ripper romance novel, folklorist Elizabeth Reynard recreated the scene of their first tryst in her in her 1930 book *The Narrow Land:* "Black Bellamy made masterful love, sailorman love that remembers how a following wind falls short and makes way while it blows."

The virile, black-haired Lothario and the fifteen-year-old with the golden locks made a dramatic couple. Reynard concluded: "Love was settled between them in no time at all, under the apple tree by the Burying Acre, and Sam sailed away with a promise to Maria that when he returned he would wed her . . . and in a sloop, laden with treasure, carry her back to the Spanish Indies, there to be made princess of a West Indian isle."

The legend of the witch and the pirate was born in an apple orchard in Eastham in the summer of 1715. But who seduced whom? Did Maria bewitch Sam? Is this how the rumor that she was the daughter of a Salem witch began? Or, did he, like the snake in the Garden of Eden, take advantage of a young girl's naïveté and devour the virgin? Whether it was love or lust, the outcome was the same: Maria was pregnant.

Affairs did happen in eighteenth-century Puritan New England. Consummation often preceded the commitment of vows, and estimates for the rate of out-of-wedlock pregnancies approached 25 percent. In 1692, to deal with the economic repercussions of such situations, Massachusetts passed an act that mandated that ". . . despite his denial, a man who was accused by a woman under oath at the time of her travail would be adjudged the father of the child and be responsible for its support with the mother, thus relieving the town of the child's care."

The same Massachusetts Act of 1692 also punished the fallen woman. If found guilty of fornication, she was subject to fines and a public whipping. The issue of an out-of-wedlock pregnancy could be rectified if it was immediately followed by marriage, not necessarily to the father of the unborn child. Convention required a wedding. Maria broke with convention—she would remain unwed, have her baby, and wait for Sam.

Like the fictional protagonist Hester Prynne in Nathaniel Hawthorne's novel *The Scarlet Letter,* Maria refused to name the father of her child. Certainly, her parents, said to be well-to-do Yarmouth farmers, would have suspected if they had seen Maria sneaking off to the tavern to be with Sam. They would never have approved of a man with no prospects.

Sam was also a very persuasive fellow. At the tavern, with Maria by his side, he hooked up with Palgrave Williams, a man of means, a jeweler. Williams listened eagerly to Bellamy's get-rich-quick scheme and offered to procure a ship. Together, they would scoop up the glittering gold and silver coins lying in the shallow waters off of Florida. Williams had one stipulation: he would serve as Quartermaster and be in charge of counting and dividing equal shares of the anticipated wealth. Of course, they would be rich beyond their wildest imagination. Bellamy and Williams assembled a crew in less than three weeks.

The lovers continued their passionate trysts as preparations were underway. Maria may have shared the secret of her pregnancy with Sam, which would have provided him with ample incentive to return quickly. With the gold salvaged from the wrecked Spanish fleet, he would have abundant wealth to provide for both Maria and their unborn love child. Since he would be gone only a few months, she could hide her pregnancy and wait for his triumphant return.

Bellamy, Williams, and their crew set sail. The months dragged on, and Maria began to show. She could have accepted an offer of marriage from a local farm boy interested more in her parents' thriving acreage than Maria. But, the now-clearly pregnant young girl's heart belonged to Sam, who, unbeknownst to her, was facing his own heartache.

Sam and his partner arrived at the shipwrecks too late. Spain had already hired divers who had gathered what they could. In Florida, Sam heard of the bold move of one Capt. Henry James, an English privateer who raided the Spanish fort where the salvaged treasure was stored. Sam called for a meeting of his crew. They had two options: go home broke or, like Captain James, "go on the account"—turn pirate. The vote was unanimous in favor of becoming indiscriminate looters of nations. As the black flag with skull and crossbones was hoisted, Sam was said to have declared: "Never again will you be slaves of the wealthy. From this day we are new men. Free men."

Back on the Cape, Maria gave birth to a baby boy bearing the telltale marks of his father: jet black hair and eyes as dark as coal. She hid the baby in the nearby barn of Elder John Knowles and crept out each night to feed the baby boy. Less than a week into his short life, the baby died. Whether it was from exposure to the cold and dampness or, as one dramatic rendering has it, from choking on a piece of straw, the tragedy did not end there. Farmer Knowles found the baby and laid in wait for the return of the child's mother. When the unsuspecting Maria returned to care for her child, Knowles accused her of infanticide. The town's selectmen ordered her confined to an Eastham prison to await trial. Maria proved as "wild as the Nauset wind;" no sooner had the iron key clicked in the lock than Maria wriggled free.

Her recapture proved to be an easy task. The sheriff would check the apple orchard, and if he didn't find her sitting there, knees clasped to her chest, then he would go a short distance further and apprehend the slight figure on the dunes silhouetted against the sea. Rumors started to fly about her escapades. Maria was either casting a spell on her jailers, bewitching them to gain her freedom, or she had signed a pact with the devil, selling her soul in exchange for the promise of being reunited with her beloved.

High on the cliffs of Wellfleet, Maria kept watch for Sam's sails.

The sheriff tired of the chase. The case never went to trial, and the town's people wanted her gone from their community. She was stoned away from Eastham as a witch. Such was the paranoia of the time. Unlike Salem, the Cape did not hang its witches. Stoning or a whipping at the stocks provided sufficient punishment. Maria had no illusions that she would ever be able to live among her family, relatives, or friends again. She retreated to an abandoned hut near the shoreline of what is now Marconi Beach in Wellfleet. High on the cliffs she could keep watch to the east for the first sign of Sam's sails. It would be a long wait.

Following their disappointment in Florida, Bellamy and Williams teamed up with pirate captain Henry Jennings. The band of pirates headed to Cuba and encountered the *Ste. Marie,* a French merchant ship with a cargo of twenty-eight thousand Spanish pieces of eight. Bellamy double-crossed Jennings and, in a daring raid, captured the heavily armed *Ste. Marie.* From Cuba, Bellamy, along with

Williams, set up a base of operations off the coast of Belize in Central America. There they picked up a New England Native American tribal member, John Julian, as their newest pirate cohort and guide. They then joined forces with Benjamin Hornigold, a master of the pirate arts. Hornigold took a liking to the young upstart and gave Bellamy the *Marianne,* a New England-built, single-decked sloop capable of carrying forty tons of booty. The *Marianne* was Bellamy's first real pirate ship.

On the high seas in June of 1716, the flotilla of pirates surrounded a ship flying the English flag. Some pirates have scruples. Hornigold, an Englishman, decreed that his fellow pirates could confiscate the liquor on board but not the cargo. Bellamy and Hornigold argued. The crew took a vote. Hornigold was outvoted in favor of Bellamy's leadership. Capt. Black Bellamy began ruling the seas. Over the course of the next twelve months, Bellamy and his crew took booty from fifty-two ships from an array of nations. In September 1716, the captured ship *Sultana* became Bellamy's new flagship. Williams, his steadfast partner, captained the *Marianne.*

In February of 1717, after giving chase for three days, they captured their biggest prize yet—the *Whydah,* a three-hundred-ton galley. Captained by Lawrence Prince, the *Whydah* engaged in the lucrative slave trade. Capt. Prince had just sold his illicit cargo of six hundred slaves and was on the homeward leg of his journey. When Bellamy boarded the *Whydah,* he found hundreds of elephant tusks, bags of lapis-blue dye, sacks of sugar, and casks of molasses. Deep in the hold, the stunned crew uncovered sacks of silver and gold, African Akan gold jewelry, and, according to rumor, a small casket of East Indian jewels with a ruby the size of a hen's egg. It was by far the biggest single haul made by pirates in the Caribbean in decades.

As Sam's fortunes rose, his erstwhile lover's plummeted. Ostracized and alone, she often dreamed that her Sam was walking across the waters to fetch her. Her hallucinations conjured up images of a flotilla of ghost ships slipping through the fog, with Sam at the helm of the flagship. In her nightmares, a slick, well-dressed man brandishing a gold-tipped cane stood over her—the devil exacting his due.

Maria survived on fish and fowl from the nearby ponds and forest. In exchange for bread and supplies, she took in weaving. Although people continued to think her a witch who danced on Sabbath nights in the hollow by the Burying Acre, a witch who had signed a pact with the devil for Sam's soul, no woman on the peninsula could weave patterns as intricate as Goody Hallett. (Goody was a term of address akin to Mrs., and the women of Eastham were more comfortable limiting their interactions to strictly formal ones.) Casual small talk did not enter into the conversation when trading with the witch. Since there was no chit-chat or gossip, Goody Hallett remained ignorant about her lover's unlawful actions.

In the spring of 1717, the *Whydah* groaned as her bow turned to the north. After eighteen months at sea, it was time to divide the spoils, repair the boats, and plan for the future. The *Whydah*'s hull, as along with that of the *Marianne,* was filled to capacity with precious treasure from around the globe. But even as they headed for the colonies, perhaps with Cape Cod as a final destination, Bellamy ordered his crew to continue to plunder. Without warning, winds from a frigid nor'easter collided with a warm and moist southern wind. The greatest storm to hit the Cape, fueled by winds as high as eighty miles per hour, seas cresting at forty to fifty feet, and zero visibility, rendered navigation useless. First, the *Marianne* grounded on the shoals, and then the *Whydah* hit a sandbar five hundred yards from shore. Buried by tons of water, the *Whydah* rolled over. Sailors were swept out to sea or crushed to death under the weight of falling cannons and sacks of gold.

To Goody Hallett, it was just another shipwreck among the thousands that occurred along the graveyard coastline of the lower Cape. She, like the other town folk, stepped over bodies that washed ashore, seeking to salvage whatever goods might be among the debris. It was only after she turned to take her meager findings back to her hut that she overhead the names of the doomed ship and its pirate captain, Black Sam Bellamy. Even if she thought one of the battered corpses might have been Sam, she would have found it nearly impossible to recognize his features after the relentless sea and pounding surf disfigured and maimed the bodies.

Tallies vary slightly as to the number of dead and missing. Over the course of several days of diving and excavation, *Whydah* salvager Barry Clifford analyzed that there were 146 men on board: 130 pirates and 16 prisoners. Only 2 were known to have survived. Neither of these was Bellamy. Washed up on the beach were 102 bodies, leaving 44 unaccounted for.

This haunted tale survives at the crossroads of fact and fantasy, the junction of legend and lore. Some say that for the rest of her days, Maria Hallett returned to the beach, but never found Sam or peace. She went mad; her wails and screeches were heard for miles. Maria's body was found on the beach. She committed suicide by slitting her throat, but her terrible anguish did not die with her. Maria's ghost walks the cliffs of Wellfleet and begs for answers.

Like all good folklore, there's always a twist. In another version, after Sam went down with his ship, his enduring love for the enchanting Eastham girl lived on. His ghost returns to reunite with the ever-faithful spirit of Maria. To those who claim to witness the apparitions on Marconi beach, the courtship flourishes. Sam's spirit rides the crest of a wave rolling into shore. He seeks the fragile shape of his love and comforts her. Together, the phantom couple stroll the beach, two ghostly forms melding into one.

Some oral history accounts say that a few weeks after the wreck, a dark-haired stranger showed up at the tavern. He had a deep scar across his forehead. When he spoke, his words were muddled and confused. He seemed to be seeking something or someone. The disheveled stranger was tolerated at the tavern because of his ability to pay for his ale. Like a magician pulling a rabbit out of his hat, the peculiar man would pluck silver or a gold coin from a dirty girdle bound tightly to his waist. Then, the stranger abruptly disappeared.

Rumors flew—the stranger must have been Black Sam Bellamy. He had survived—so strong was his love for Maria that even stunned by a blow to the head and tossed roughly ashore, his mind clung to only the thought of finding the girl he left behind. More rumors circulated. A proper Puritan matron repeated to all who would listen that as she had approached Goody Hallett's hut in the days prior to her suicide, she heard a male and female voice arguing. Offended by the vile language, she did not enter the hut to deliver wool for Goody to weave nor ascertain who was inside. She turned away and hastened to her home in Eastham.

There were dark undertones and malevolent forces at work. Maria had delivered a child alone, and mourned its death. She had been arrested, accused of fornication and infanticide, jailed and stoned out of town as a witch and a whore—all before reaching her sixteenth birthday. The gossip mongers claimed her pact with the devil was not for Sam's safe return but rather for revenge on the man who had abandoned her. Like the legendary sea witch of Billingsgate who created havoc for sailors on the high seas, Maria joined in cursing every man, especially Sam, who so cavalierly left their womenfolk behind. In exchange for her soul, Maria asked the devil for power to control the sea. Indeed, the *Whydah* went down in the fiercest nor'easter ever to hit the Cape.

"I have no doubt that Goody had a hand in brewing the April hurricane that brought on disaster to Bellamy's ship, the *Whidah*," declared Jeremiah Digges. Digges was the pen name for Joseph Berger, who wrote about Goody Hallet in *Cape Cod Pilot*, a 1937 compilation of the Federal Writers Project.

After salvaging whatever treasure she could from what was scattered on the beach, Maria befriended one of the survivors, Indian John. In exchange for hiding him from the authorities, the Indian confided in Maria that in the hours before the wreck, each man on board had stuffed his pockets and girdled a cloth around his waist with as much gold and silver coins as they could grab. He knew where the other survivors have hidden their secret cache.

The mysterious stranger might not have been as befuddled as he appeared. He sought news of any recovered treasure from the *Whydah*. On learning that Maria was living in a hut and that a man with the features of an Indian might be hiding nearby, the stranger confronted Maria. Both had aged considerably. Maria's once silken hair was matted and dirty, her blue eyes sunken and hollow. This is not the delicate, fair-skinned beauty of whom he dreamt during so many long nights at sea. The woman before him had wrinkles and blemishes, skin spotted like worn brown leather. This was a foul-smelling, angry creature whose features contorted at the sight of *him,* a sallow, sickly man, not the dashing figure of her innocent youth. Gouges and scars marred his face, arms, and hands. His teeth were rotting and yellow. Gray streaks cut through dull black hair.

The meeting ended in a shouting match. He demanded the return of his treasure. She screamed that he will never see one more coin in his lifetime. He drew a short, sharp-edged knife. She produced an equally vicious blade hidden in her ample bodice. Both suffered fatal wounds. In the dim pre-dawn light, a lone fisherman, walking the beach below the cliffs, stumbled over two bodies.

On Marconi Beach in Wellfleet, two angry wraiths are locked in battle. On stormy nights, the pounding waves toss this phantom pair on to the beach. They emerge from the dingy foam tangled together, almost indistinguishable from the other flotsam and jetsam if not for the screeches and screams that envelop them.

One haunted tale of a pirate and his would-be bride provides a choice of various endings: the wailing ghost of Maria, mad and alone; the reunited spirits of lovers Sam and Maria; and the angry wraiths—the pirate and the witch—at each other's throats.

Lagniappe: Barry Clifford, who discovered the wreck of the pirate ship *Whydah,* Ken Kinkor, late historian at the Whydah Museum in Provincetown, and a host of other researchers, folklorists, and writers all agree that Black Sam Bellamy was the most daring and successful pirate of the eighteenth century. The love story of Sam and Maria, while passed down from generation to generation for nearly three hundred years, is a bit harder to authenticate. Maria Hallett is the true unknown in this equation. Her starring role defies attempts to document her existence. She is most often referred to as Maria Hallett, and later, after her stoning in Eastham and her escape to her Wellfleet hut, as Goody Hallett. As pointed out by Clifford, Kinkor, and biographer Kathleen Brunelle, Maria was an unusual name for Puritan New England, as it was more often associated with families

A mysterious necklace of gold beads, kept by a Mary Hallett.

of a predominately Catholic region. The Halletts of Cape Cod had no daughters by the name of Maria. Mary, Mercy, Mehitable are among those listed in Hallett genealogy records. During his exhaustive research, historian Kinkor uncovered an important document related to one Mary Hallet, born 1693 and never married.

In her will, dated April 1751, Mary Hallet divided all her worldly possessions among her surviving sisters, brothers, nieces, and nephews, with one remarkable exception—a string of priceless gold beads. The will reads in part: "I give and bequeath to my sister, Hope Griffith, my wearing appearell, including two gold rings but not my gold beads." This Mary Hallett is very attached to her prized piece of jewelry, and it seem that she took the necklace with her to the grave. It is unlikely that a proper unmarried woman of this era would have received such an unusual and expensive necklace as a gift. The beads were not passed down from her family, as there is no record of them in her parents' estate. Were these golden beads part of the *Whydah* treasure?

If Mary Hallett of Yarmouth was the Maria Hallett of legend, then the ghostly pair who haunts Marconi Beach could not be the eternally wrathful spirits but rather the loving couple, reunited. Barry Clifford would prefer to think that the tale of the two lovers is true. "It's one of the things that caught my attention as a young person . . . it's a Cape folk story that I've always liked to believe."

The Whydah *and its pirate treasure wrecked in a storm off of Cape Cod.*
(Photograph by Russell Sillery)

24

The Ghosts of the Whydah Expedition

I have learned to expect the unexpected, but I still find it hard to deal with the unexplained. Things that go bump in the night are bothersome to me, not because they are frightening, but because I don't know how they happen or why.

—Barry Clifford, *Expedition Whydah*

For most New Englanders, Thanksgiving is celebrated as a time to reflect and be grateful. For salvager Barry Clifford, Thanksgiving 1981 was the start of a grueling quest. Dinner that year was at the home of Pulitzer Prize-winning author William Styron. Over after-dinner drinks, Clifford shared the tantalizing tale of the wreck of the pirate ship *Whydah*. As his passion for the story of Capt. Black Sam Bellamy unfolded, a fellow guest, a legendary CBS news anchor, was intrigued: "It was Walter Cronkite, and he asked me what I was doing about it. I told him I was thinking about going to look for a shipwreck on the Cape called the *Whydah*." Cronkite threw down the gauntlet. "Why don't you do it?"

After an unrelenting saga on land and sea, Barry Clifford did just that. The *Whydah,* a former slave ship captured by pirate Sam Bellamy, is the only authenticated pirate shipwreck ever found, and her treasures are still being recovered—with a few nudges from the spirit world.

In April 1983, Clifford set up his land-based operations at the Captain Heman Smith House, a two-story colonial near Jeremiah's Gutter in Orleans. Jeremiah's Gutter was the first canal to cut across the Cape peninsula, connecting Cape Cod Bay to the Atlantic Ocean. Prior to his salvage crew's arrival, Clifford had a haunting dream: Emerging from the muck of Jeremiah's Gutter was a parade of ragged men. If the proximity to the Gutter crept into Clifford's subconscious it produced some intimidating imagery of men dressed like pirates and covered with seaweed and sand. The menacing phantoms strode across the lawn of the Captain house, barged through the front door, stomped single file up the stairs to Clifford's room, and shoved the door open. Jarred from sleep, Clifford flipped on the light fully expecting to see ". . . a room full of pirates protesting the fact that I was searching for their booty," but the room was devoid of phantoms. The bedroom door remained securely closed. There were no telltale muddy footprints or slimy strands of seaweed. Nothing to indicate that the pirate ghosts existed ". . . anywhere but in my head."

Still, the images lingered. Deciphering the meaning of any dream or nightmare is always a toss-up. Either the grim ghosts were hostile and didn't want Clifford to search for the booty they had worked so

The Whydah Museum houses the artifacts brought up from the wreck.

hard for, or the spirited pirates from the past were welcoming him to their watery lair. At the time, Clifford elected to take a positive view, believing that this was an invitation to search for the *Whydah*. Looking back on the decades-old dream of phantom pirates tracking him down, the successful discoverer of the wreck of the *Whydah* shrugs it off. "I guess I was just thinking about them."

Today, sitting in his private quarters on the second floor over the Whydah Museum on MacMillan Wharf in Provincetown, Barry Clifford is a striking presence. A shaved head emphasizes piercing sea-blue eyes. A black tee-shirt shows off a diver's well-toned physique molded by thirty-plus years on the open water. His ship, the *Vast Explorer*, a gleaming white sixty-five-foot vessel, is tied to the dock below. Clifford is impatient. Now that he has found the *Whydah*, his focus is on the on-going excavation. The 2013 season could promise a peek at the mother lode of Bellamy's treasure. Barry Clifford is guarded about what is next on the agenda.

Seeking a pirate shipwreck and her scattered treasure lost for more than 250 years in the ever-shifting sands of an undersea world is a daunting undertaking. Wading through a sea of ancient court documents, records, and obscure maps to pinpoint the location is equally frustrating. In the early stages of the research process, Clifford became a man obsessed. Skeptics saw him as a dreamer, out of touch with reality. Clifford readily admits he had his moments. In his book about the expedition, several inexplicable incidents are revealed.

In attempting to recall the events, Clifford said he had a lot on his mind at the time. His thoughts had drifted to the Capt. Cyprian Southack, the eighteenth-century captain appointed by the British governor to recover treasure from the wreck of the *Whydah*. Southack recovered bodies from the beach, but failed to retrieve any treasure. While driving around one morning, Clifford pulled up to a stoplight, and an image of the scowling face of Captain Southhack materialized inches from his own. The phantom figure seemed to be holding a map in his hand as he scanned the land for familiar landmarks. A honking of a car horn behind him interrupted Clifford's reverie, and the ghostly searcher dissipated.

A scale model of Black Sam Bellamy's ship is on display in the museum.

While a chance to have a conversation with Capt. Southack eluded him, another ghost hung around long enough to offer a few valuable clues. Again expressing reluctance to dwell on ghostly images, Clifford remembers a second vivid dream. He and Black Sam Bellamy were standing on the deck of a ship. Beneath them, the ocean had an eerie stillness, a dead calm. Abruptly, a soundtrack kicked in: laughter punctuated by high-decibel screams from a cacophony of disembodied voices was immediately followed by a dialogue between the twenty-first-century explorer and the 1717 ghost captain. Initially, the spirit of Black Sam responded with only a disdainful leer when asked if they were closing in on the wreck of the *Whydah*. The imposing phantom nodded in the affirmative, and then spoke in a brusque voice: "You are close, but too close to shore." This was followed by another hint that things are "not what they used to be." The combination of these clues, although veiled and vague, propelled Clifford awake. Despite the three a.m. predawn hour, he called Stretch Grey, his trusted captain, and shouted into the phone, "I know where the *Whydah* is!" Grey hung up on him. Clifford redialed. In a rush of words he blurted that the wreck was farther out. In his dream, Sam Bellamy ". . . told me where to look."

Clifford relates that when the rest of the crew heard about his alleged conversation with the long-dead pirate, they thought he had finally gone insane. They insisted the search continue where they were presently anchored near shore. The first season of searching for the *Whydah* ended in defeat. Unfazed, Clifford remained steadfast in his conviction that psycho-imaging, which he defines as using ". . . paranormal methods to find artifacts instead of the magnetometer," would be an asset in their quest during a resumed search the following year.

On July 20, 1984, during the second season, an NBC camera crew was on board the *Vast Explorer*. The sky was nearly clear—only one small cloud hovered on the horizon. The plan was to get footage as the divers searched a new site. Having come up empty-handed at fifty other sites, the mood topside bordered on hopelessness. A diver went down. He reappeared in a flash, as if he had seen a shark or the looming ghost of Sam Bellamy. His discovery was better than a phantom pirate—the diver had spotted three cannons. A second diver pulled up a cannon ball encrusted with a gold coin, a Spanish piece of eight with markings dating it to 1688. With proof that the *Whydah* was below them, the mood turned jubilant. Overhead, the small dark cloud moved stealthily to a position directly over the boat. There was a bright flash of lighting and deafening clap of thunder. One startled crew member proclaimed, "It's Sam Bellamy!" Captain Grey added a terse observation that the pirates didn't want to be found.

Clifford remembers the odd weather phenomenon. "Just right after we found the shipwreck, you know, a thunderstorm came over the top of the ship . . . it was a turning point for us, the thunderstorm. I guess you could extrapolate that into anything, but it just happened at the time we found the wreck. Yeah, I would say a strange coincidence."

After the mini-storm passed, the divers recovered a glittering hoard

Strange things continued to happen on Vast Explorer, *Clifford's research vessel.*

A pewter plate and spoon were among the everyday artifacts recovered from the debris field.

of gold and silver coins. In one twenty-minute period, Clifford alone brought up 280 coins. Clifford says that he wanted to hold them close, not for their value, but for the secrets they surely held. These were the very reason the men had turned pirates.

Everyday items—pewter plates, forks, spoons, a tankard—underscored the human connection. One item—a leather shoe with the leg bone still attached—sent shock waves through the crew. Protected from decay by concretion from a cannon that had pinned the doomed sailor to the sea floor, the size-five men's shoe with its silk stocking was of a style worn by someone from the upper class, not your average pirate. "It was years later that we were able to decipher that," states Clifford.

After the discovery of the shoe and leg bone, the *Whydah* research director, the late Ken Kinkor, began poring over primary source documents. In a 1716 Antigua court deposition, Capt. Abijah Savage testified that his passenger ship, the *Bonetta,* was overtaken by the pirate ship *Marianne,* then captained by Sam Bellamy. For fifteen days, the pirates plundered and intimidated the passengers, taking away anything of value. Two of the *Bonetta*'s crew switched allegiance and joined the pirates. One small boy watched in wonder, then announced he was going, too. Young John King was traveling with his mother from Antigua to Jamaica. John's mother refused her son's request. However, the willful child prevailed. According to Captain Savage, the boy was neither forced nor coerced. "He declared he would Kill himself if he was Restrained, and even threatened his Mother who was then on Board as a passenger with Deponent."

Clifford shakes his head in genuine puzzlement. "I was wondering why he would threaten his mother and join the pirate crews—and what kind of a mother she was. The question is: What was going on aboard the pirate ship that looked so exciting for him? So, he must have seen things going on on the pirate ship that attracted him if the primary source documents are correct." When Sam Bellamy replaced the *Marianne* with the *Whydah* as his flag ship, the littlest pirate, John King, went along.

The shoe and leg bone sat in storage until Kinkor had the bone

Black Sam Bellamy proudly flew the Jolly Roger on the Whydah.

examined by the Center for Historical Archaeology and the Smithsonian Institution. The examinations confirmed the bone to be that of a child between the ages of eight and eleven. To date, no other historical records have revealed that a child so young was allowed to sign up with a nefarious band of buccaneers. In trying to picture what it was like the day little John King sealed his fate, Kinkor speculated that Bellamy must have admired his spirit. "I could almost see him begging Bellamy to let him join, and Bellamy not having the heart to refuse him." A human artifact, like this child's shoe, serves as a chilling reminder of the perils of a pirate's life.

While a total of 12,107 artifacts were brought to the surface during the second season, doubters remained. The artifacts proved that this was the wreck of an eighteenth-century ship, but not necessarily the *Whydah.* Shifting sands or devious phantom pirates at work had hidden the physical evidence needed in a pit forty-five feet deep. The *Whydah's* cast bronze bell, indisputable proof that this wreck was indeed the tomb of pirates who sailed with Black Sam Bellamy, did not come to the surface until the summer of 1985. With it came a surprise. Until the encrustations fell away, the spelling of the name of Bellamy's ship had been recorded in documents as "Whidah." Nearly three centuries later, the error would be corrected. The name, *THE WHYDAH GALLY 1716,* was emblazoned around the upper band of the bell. The headline on the November 1, 1985, edition of the *New York Times* proclaimed, "Bell Confirms That Salvors Found Pirate Ship of Legend." The bell, as reported in the article, declared that this was "The first identification in history of a pirate ship." Still, the troublesome ghosts did not fade quietly into the night, nor did the operation proceed on an even keel.

The salvage operation continued, but the number of recovered artifacts dwindled. Expenses mounted: preservation costs, administrative overhead, equipment maintenance and repairs. Clifford argued valiantly that they had not yet hit the mother lode. The investors grumbled, lost faith, and pulled the plug. Despite all the success and notoriety, the site was closed. The doomed souls of the *Whydah* could return to their watery grave and be hassle free.

Still, Barry Clifford could not let go. In 1998, almost fourteen years after locating the bell, this underwater explorer and avid preservationist resumed operations—and the aggravated pirates appeared to fire a few warning shots across his bow. On the first attempt out to the site, an engine malfunction triggered an onboard scramble to make repairs. With the engine finally running, a thick fog rolled in, limiting visibility to less than one hundred yards. Glitches in the new GPS blocked the crew from plotting coordinates of the artifacts on the site map. Resigned to their fate that this trip was a no-go, they made a U-turn back to the dock—with near-disastrous results. In the impenetrable fog, they relied on the GPS, which misdirected them straight into the shallow waters of the shore. The hull of the research vessel hit bottom. Clifford assessed their narrow escape from disaster. Without fast reaction time, powerful engines allowing them to reverse course, and a large helping of luck, they would have ended up on the same beach as Bellamy and his crew. It appeared as if the doomed pirates were toying with the crew of the *Vast,* giving them a glimpse of what they had faced in those final fatal moments—a cruel taunt from beyond the grave.

Clifford's passion to be on "the trail of something big" was palpable. He was convinced they would find the *Whydah* when "the pirates thought we had earned it." Recalling the details of the averted catastrophe with the flawed GPS, Clifford points out that, "It was thirty years ago. It happens a lot . . . a couple of years ago our rudder broke and we turned around and headed into shore. There's been a bunch of incidents like that."

A new member of the team, Chris Macort, was convinced that the pirates were trying to establish communications. Macort had been aboard the *Crumpstey,* their back-up vessel, when the radio began to crackle. Cutting through the static was a voice. He cranked up the volume to hear demands: "We want your boat. We want your boat." On the next visit to the site, Macort brought along a bottle of rum, announcing that he had figured out what the pirates craved, and poured the contents of the bottle into the ocean swells.

A broad smile lights up the face of expedition leader Clifford as he recalls the ritual. "That was just one of those fun things that you do. Chris poured some rum into the water just to, you know, appease the pirates." The offering was well received. That season was one of the best ever. Divers sucked up a river of gold dust with a turkey baster and brought to the surface a grinding stone and a rare swivel cannon.

Strange things continued to happen. In July 1998, Clifford and crew were accompanied by photographers and a writer from the *National Geographic.* Unfortunately, visibility below was poor, and the underwater photographers were frustrated. There would be one last try in the morning. That night, the pirates paid another spirited call. Those sleeping below decks awoke at two a. m. to a terrifying crash and piercing scream, as if someone had fallen or was pushed overboard. A head count showed that all eleven people on the *Vast Explorer* were accounted for. The next thought was that another boat had collided with the *Crumpstey,* the whaler tied behind the *Vast.* A flashlight inspection showed all was well. Another bloodcurdling scream split the air. Crewmate Macort was convinced this time that it wasn't the intimidation factor of the pirates of the *Whydah* but rather Captain Crumpstey's irate ghost. Crumpstey had been captain of the *Marianne,* a ship laden with seven thousand gallons of Maderia wine that the pirates of the *Whydah* had confiscated for their own pleasure. To placate the enraged captain, Macort repeated his new-found alcoholic ritual. He poured a bottle of wine over the waters, and the screaming stopped.

In the morning, it was Macort's turn to dive. At thirty-two feet, the youthful diver found a long, curving section of the *Whydah*'s hull. A portion of the bulkhead was lined with metal. It was the gunpowder room near what would have been Sam Bellamy's quarters. When Clifford dove down to inspect the astonishing find, his thoughts gravitated inevitably to the men, the most successful pirates of their time, who went down with the ship: "This was their tomb."

Through years of agonizing trial and error, success and disappointments, a roller coaster of emotions, a philosophical Clifford summed up his feelings in *Expedition Whydah:* "I was not insane or irrational for believing that the spirits of the dead buccaneers looked over the wreck of their ship . . . taking another man's booty isn't supposed to be easy . . . eventually you have to contend with the real owners."

Lagniappe: Housed in a colonial-era home on Main Street in Wellfleet, Aesop's Tables was a popular Cape Cod restaurant. Centuries earlier, Sam Bellamy may well have passed this spot as he strolled through town. In 1998, Barry Clifford, some of his crew, and the crew from the National Geographic had just finished dinner the night before they went out on the *Vast Explorer* and subsequently discovered the hull of the *Whydah*. After they left, an incident occurred that raises many eyebrows. A man, eating dinner alone at the far end of the bar, went to the restroom. He came out white and shaking. He announced that he had to leave the restaurant immediately. His server asked what was wrong. "You might think I am going crazy here, but I just saw a ghost in your bathroom." The frightened man said the ghost was a young woman with pale blond hair and an ability to make the room frigid in July. His description of the female apparition matched the profile often attributed to Maria Hallett, Black Sam Bellamy's lover. The agitated patron signed the credit card slip and made a quick exit. The waitress repeated what he said to her manager. The manager followed up. He went into the bathroom to check it out, and found nothing. He asked the waitress for the name of her customer. She flipped through her receipts. "Here it is—the name is Bellamy." Aesop's Tables closed in 2004. The historic former captain's house has reopened as Winslow's Tavern. There have been no recent reports of a lovely female ghost startling guests in the bathroom.

The Whydah Museum in Provincetown preserves and houses the artifacts salvaged from the *Whydah*. For all those who have ever harbored a secret yearning to uncover their own sunken treasure, this museum will transport you into Sam Bellamy's world and allow you to view the treasures hidden for almost three centuries in the sea bottom off Cape Cod. However, Clifford is adamant about not applying the term "treasure hunter" to his work. "Treasure hunters sell treasure. We've never sold any treasure. The project is about archeology—digging up the ships, preserving the ships for posterity and for historical reasons." As for the ghosts of the *Whydah*, he is less rigid: "For fun, I'll talk about a ghost thing, but it's not something I spend a lot of time thinking about."

The Old Burying Ground in Truro.

Epilogue

It is wonderful that five thousand years have now elapsed since the creation of the world, and still is undecided whether or not there has ever been an instance of the spirit of any person appearing after death. All argument is against it; but all belief is for it.

—Samuel Johnson

Samuel Johnson, an eighteenth-century poet, essayist, moralist, literary critic, creator of the dictionary, and lauded as "the most distinguished man of letters in English history," could not render a definitive verdict for or against ghosts. Three centuries later, we are no closer to the answer. We are left to rely on our own experiences, those of family, friends, and passing acquaintances. We choose to accept or reject the validity of many an oft-told tale.

Then, there are those tales told with such truth and sincerity that all doubt vanishes. When an antiquarian book collector and dealer speaks of the specter who sits on his bed, you listen. When an award-winning chef lists the ghosts who have followed her through the years, you're intrigued. When the upstanding members of a Congregational church swear that their first minister continues to express his disapproval with some poltergeist activity inside their house of worship, skepticism slips away.

Will there ever be a day when we'll know with absolute certainty that spirits of the dead can slip back and forth between our world and theirs? For Sheila FitzGerald, owner of the Old Yarmouth Inn who believes she caught her dogs interacting with an unseen presence, it's proof enough. Malcom Perna of the Colonial Inn keeps a ghost ledger and tracks his guests' ghostly encounters. He relies on the math—the number of correct matches of ghosts to haunted rooms is sufficient motivation to keep the paranormal study going. Bill Putman has only one ghost to look after, and he is satisfied that little Susan is happy at the Simmons Homestead. The Sandwich Glass Museum created holograms of Rebecca and William Burgess, giving visitors the illusion that this couple still yearn and grieve for each other. The love story of Maria Hallett and Sam Bellamy is one of the most enduring legends on Cape Cod.

Whether they are born from a need to believe that death is not the end and that some form of life endures, haunted tales make the implausible seem true. They impart a sense of hope, a connection to the past—and that will do for now.

As a "washashore," a newcomer to the Cape and the islands, I had much to learn. I am grateful to the many generous residents who shared their stories with me: Derek Bartlett, Karyn Caliri, Stephen Caliri, Anne Carlson, Barry Clifford, Bill Conway, Shelly Conway, Sheila FitzGerald, Jana Hamby, Susan Jarrell, Ken Kinkor, Bob Lehman, Ed Maas, Ruth Manchester, Marianne McCaffery, Barbara Milligan, Malcom Perna, Bill Putnam, Pam Roehm, Ed Sabin, Shirley Sabin, Craig Spery, Mary Beth Splaine, Hugh Blair-Smith, David Troutman, Arpad Voros, Jim Visbeck, Bryan Webb, and everyone who added their own special twist to the tales.

Additional thanks to the National Park Service and the Nantucket Historical Association. To all the librarians and staff at the Masphee Public Library, thank you, thank you, thank you for helping to track down reference books and source material. This fantastic facility also hosts a wonderful non-fiction writers' group. To my colleagues at the Cape Cod Writer's Center: Ben Gagnon, Joe Nugent, and especially Hugh Blair-Smith—your critiques and reviews were invaluable.

A special thank you to friends and family for their continued support: my brother, Russell Sillery, for his haunting images of Maria and Sam and the pirate ship; my son-in-law, Tim Moore, who answered endless questions about architecture; my daughters, Danielle Genter Moore, Rebecca Genter, and Heather Genter; and Michael and Leila Sillery Moore, for allowing Baba time out from playtime to write.

Appendix

For more information about the historic sites in this book, or to take a personal tour, the following is a list of their locations on Cape Cod and the nearby islands of Martha's Vineyard and Nantucket.

Aquinnah Cultural Center
35 Aquinnah Circle
Aquinnah, MA 02535

Barnstable House
3010 Main Street
Barnstable, MA 02630

Barnstable Restaurant and Tavern
3176 Main Street
Barnstable, MA 02630

Bramble Inn
2019 Main Street
Brewster, MA 02631

Captain Linnell House
137 Skaket Beach Road
Orleans, MA 02653

Church of the New Jerusalem
260 Route 6A
Yarmouth Port, MA 02675

Colonial House Inn
277 Main Street, Route 6A
Yarmouth Port, MA 02675

Cove Burying Ground
Route 6A and Pine Woods Road
Eastham, MA 02642

Crocker Tavern House
3095 Main Street
Barnstable, MA 02630

Daggett House
59 North Water Street
Edgartown, MA 02539

Edward Gorey House
8 Strawberry Lane
Yarmouth Port, MA 02675

Highfield Hall and Gardens
56 Highfield Drive
Falmouth, MA 02540

Highfield Theatre/Falmouth Theatre Guild
58 Highfield Drive
Falmouth, MA 02540

Isaiah Thomas Books
4632 Falmouth Road
Cotuit, MA 02635

Jared Coffin House
29 Broad Street
Nantucket, MA 02554

John Pope House (Tupper Inn)
110 Tupper Road
Sandwich, MA 02563

Ocean Edge Resort and Golf Club
2907 Main Street
Brewster, MA 02631

Old Jail
3353 Main Street/Route 6A
Barnstable, MA 02630

Old South Church/Second Congregational Meeting House
11 Orange Street
Nantucket, MA 02554

Old Yarmouth Inn
223 Route 6A
Yarmouth Port, MA 02675

Orleans Waterfront Inn
3 Old Country Road
Orleans, MA 02653

Penniman House
Fort Hill Road and Governor Prence Road
Eastham, MA 02642

Provincetown Library
356 Commercial Street
Provincetown, MA 02657

Roberts House Inn
11 India Street
Nantucket, MA 02554

Sandwich Glass Museum
129 Main Street
Sandwich, MA 02563

Scargo Café
799 Main Street
Dennis, MA 02638

Scargo Tower
152 Scargo Hill Road
Dennis, MA 02638

Simmons Homestead Inn
288 Scudder Avenue
Hyannis Port, MA 02601

Truro Meeting House/First Congregational Parish of Truro
3 First Parish Lane
Truro, MA 02536

Victorian Inn
24 South Water Street
Edgartown, MA 02539

Vincent House
99 Main Street
Edgartown, MA 02539

Whydah Pirate Museum
16 MacMillian Pier
Provincetown, MA 02657